KEEPING
FOOD
FRESH

"Are you interested in home fruit and vegetable production but are turned off by the boiling, blanching
and BTUs implicit in canning and freezing? This book
contains a wealth of ideas from a European artisanal
tradition that predates those modern methods by mil-
lennia (even modern "canning" is barely 200 years old).
The French farmers and gardeners who contributed
these recipes look at food preservation as a deeply cre-
ative and enlivening process, like that used to make
cheese or fine wine.

I have been farming and pickling for twenty years,
making a portion of my income from a small farm-
stead sauerkraut business, and I am impressed by the
variety of suggestions in this book, particularly the
excellent chapter on lacto-fermentation."

—*Peter Young, co-founder of Hill Farm of Vermont*

KEEPING
FOOD
FRESH

❧ *Old World Techniques & Recipes* ❦

THE GARDENERS
AND FARMERS OF
TERRE VIVANTE

⚜ ⚜ ⚜

Chelsea Green Publishing Company
White River Junction, Vermont
Totnes, England

Printed in the United States.
First printing, August 1999.
04 03 02 01   2 3 4 5 6
Originally published in 1992 in Paris by Terre Vivante.

Library of Congress Cataloging-in-Publication Data
Conserves naturelles des quartre saisons. English.
    Keeping food fresh : old-world techniques and
    recipes : the gardeners and farmers of Terre
    Vivante.
            p.   cm.
        Includes index.
        ISBN 1-890132-10-1 (alk. paper)
        1. Food—Preservation. I. Aubert, Claude.
    II. Terre Vivante. III. Title.
    TX601.C643   1999
    641.4—dc21   99-35132
                                                CIP

Chelsea Green Publishing Company
P.O. Box 428
White River Junction, Vermont 05001
(800) 639-4099
www.chelseagreen.com

❧ CONTENTS ❧

Contents

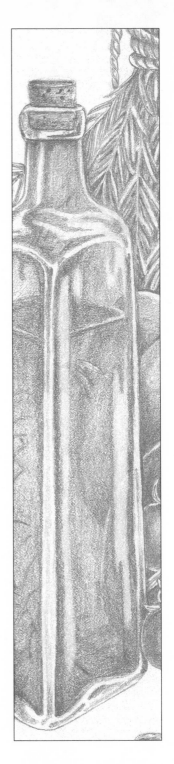

THE POETRY OF FOOD

BY ELIOT COLEMAN

I

N THE OPENING PARAGRAPHS OF HIS classic *Soil and Civilization,* Edward Hyams decries how modern misapplication of science has caused humans to "begin working across or against the grain of life." Hyams notes how science, when it becomes master rather than servant, displaces the age-old natural wisdom that has maintained the "integrity of life." Without that integrity, humans begin to lose contact with the "poet," which Hyams describes as the instinctive understanding of wholeness that has nurtured their well-being through the centuries.

Such change is abundantly evident in our modern American diet. The business of food science is in conflict with the poetry of human nourishment. Store shelves are filled with products that keep seemingly forever, such as canned or frozen food, ultra-pasteurized dairy products, devitalized flour. Irradiated food now lurks on the horizon. I prefer to live a different reality. On a recent trip to France, while shopping in small village stores, I was inspired to see other people favoring the artisanal over the industrial. The baskets of shoppers ahead of me at the counter contained fresh seasonal vegetables, fresh bread, fresh fruits, and fresh chestnuts. Not a single canned or frozen item. The preserved foods I did see people buying were similarly traditional: wine, cheese, dried fruits, and sauerkraut and pickles, sold fresh from large crocks.

Food preservation techniques can be divided into two categories: the modern scientific methods that remove the life from food, and the natural "poetic" methods that maintain or enhance the life in food. The poetic techniques produce live foods like those chosen by the French shoppers— foods that have been celebrated for centuries and are considered gourmet delights today. The scientific techniques produce dead foods and literally seal them in coffins. My instincts tell me that long-dead foods cannot properly nourish long-lived people.

If we want to be well nourished, we need to eat what I call "real food." We all know what it is. During the summer, real food is fresh from the garden or the organic farmers' market. It is grown locally and is free of all the post-harvest treatments used for foods shipped from far away. During the rest of the year, real food is fresh from cold frames and greenhouses, or is preserved by techniques that maintain and enhance its ease of digestion, nutritional status, and pleasing flavor. These are qualities that not even the most deceptive Madison Avenue advertiser could try to claim for canned or frozen foods. When we eat real food, we again work with rather than against "the grain of life."

Years ago, I sponsored and led a number of organic farming study tours to Europe. I wanted to share with American farmers the techniques and also the inspiration I had learned from the best European farmers. While we were there, enjoying meals of local products at farms and in restaurants, I imagined similar tours to study the traditional foods we were eating. After returning to the States, I was too busy with farming to ever carry out this idea, but the concept stuck with me. These were foods we needed to know more about.

I could not be more pleased to present this book as a substitute for visiting the artisans of food preservation in person. This is *real food.*

HOW THIS BOOK CAME TO BE

W HEN WE ASKED THE READERS of the French organic gardening magazine *Les Quatre Saisons du jardinage (Four-season gardening)* to share their secrets of fruit and vegetable preservation, we admit that we were somewhat skeptical. Hadn't all good recipes already been published?

Much to our surprise, we received over five hundred recipes. Many were classics; however, some were totally new, some had been adapted, and others had been regarded as common knowledge, and thus never had been published. Examples include cabbage sauce, bottled Swiss chard, lacto-fermented sweet corn, sauerkraut with whole cabbages, carob honey, layered apple paste, and sugar-free jams.

This book deliberately omits today's two most widely used methods of food preservation: freezing and canning. These techniques are covered at length in numerous other books. Moreover, we believe that the traditional methods proposed herein are superior in every way: They preserve more flavor and nutritional content, are less costly, and use less energy.

A compilation of recipes from over a hundred different authors, this book has remained faithful to the personality behind each recipe. For instance, we have kept most of the text in the first person, and have retained many of the authors' personal comments. These decisions have produced a collection of rather lively recipes that nevertheless conform with our underlying principles, since the following criteria apply throughout:

1. All preserving is done as naturally as possible, with minimal use of heat (boiling) or cold (freezing). Where recipes call for additional cooking, it is for a purpose such as preventing food contamination, or concentrating jams, jellies, and so on.
2. Maximum flavor and nutritional value are retained.
3. Methods have been tested and are easy for families to try out.
4. Ingredients are whole or minimally processed, and locally grown, apart from a few exceptions.
5. Sugar is used sparingly (in jams, jellies, and the like).

The result: 250 recipes, most of them previously unpublished, encompassing nine preservation methods, and providing readers with the means to preserve all these foods in optimal ways. Given the boundless stores of popular wisdom about food, this book hopes to make a start at "preserving" those stores for future generations.

The Editors at Terre Vivante

ABOUT TERRE VIVANTE

Terre Vivante is a nonprofit association founded in 1980 to promote a way of life that is respectful of the natural environment. Until the early 1990s, Terre Vivante's main activity was the publication of an organic gardening magazine, *Les Quatre Saisons du jardinage*. Since 1994, with the creation of a remarkable ecological education center, the work of Terre Vivante has taken on new dimensions, including:

❖ *Construction of hands-on demonstrations of numerous ecological approaches to the challenges of daily life, for instance energy-efficient buildings, organic gardens, and water-conservation methods*

❖ *A range of projects intended to contribute to the revival of a rural region, after years of decline*

❖ *Assistance and support for farmers and gardeners, particularly in the development of long-term plans to widen the popularity of ecological agricultural techniques*

The design of Centre Terre Vivante's facilities and programs is based upon "first principles"—clean air, clean water, and clean food, which used to be the birthright of all people. Although the effects of pollution can now be traced throughout the world, at Terre Vivante the malign impacts of human development are being minimized. On formerly infertile land at an altitude of more than two thousand feet above sea level, Terre Vivante's horticulturalists are growing a wide range of foods, including forgotten or endangered varieties, relying entirely upon composts and organic fertilizers generated nearby. In addition to vegetables and flowers, visitors can see a bamboo garden, nursery, playground, wild meadows, and a constructed wetlands for waste-water treatment. Terre Vivante's buildings demonstrate the potential for earth-friendly construction, utilizing passive and active solar features including photovoltaics, composting toilets, solar and wood-burning water heaters, and natural materials. The center's restaurant offers delicious meals made from locally grown ingredients, featuring many regional favorites, and has been described as having "the finest restaurant view in Europe."

The publishing program of Terre Vivante has grown beyond production of the magazine *Les Quatre Saisons* to encompass a list of more than fifty books on a diversity of subjects, including organic gardening, health and nutrition, ecological building methods, and environmental education. An ongoing series of lectures and workshops is also offered at the center, with schedules available on Terre Vivante's web site (www.terrevivante.org).

Centre Terre Vivante is open to visitors from May through October. For more information, please contact:

Terre Vivante
Domaine de Raud   telephone: 33 (0)4 76 34 80 80
BP 20—38710 Mens cedex   fax: 33 (0)4 76 34 84 02
Isère, France

A NOTE ON THE ENGLISH TRANSLATION

As explained in the Preface, this book grew out of an invitation to readers of a popular organic gardening magazine that they submit favorite (in some cases "secret") recipes for preserving fruits and vegetables. The recipes collected in this way vary widely in voice and emphasis. Since in most cases the contributors were farmers and gardeners, not professional culinarians, some of the submitted recipes are more complete than others with respect to quantities, materials, and estimates of time. We invite you to approach this book with a spirit of curiosity, adventure, and improvisation. We apologize in advance to readers who find certain aspects of some recipes imprecise. The publisher will welcome comments and suggestions, which we will do our best to accommodate in reprints of the book (Chelsea Green's address is noted on the copyright page).

In addition, readers are advised to carefully read the Note on Food Safety on page xvii. In days gone by, traditional techniques for preserving foods were taught by an experienced family member or neighbor, which allowed an apprentice to query the teacher repeatedly and thoroughly. These days, many people learn age-old techniques by reading books, which permits no such back-and-forth. Recipes should not be followed carelessly nor without common sense. When in doubt, err on the side of caution, and consult more comprehensive books about food preservation and storage, including Mike and Nancy Bubel's *Root Cellaring: Natural Cold Storage of Fruits & Vegetables* (Storey, 1991) and Janet C. Greene's *Putting Food By* (Penguin, 1992).

Editorial notes for the English edition are signaled by a fleur-de-lis (❧).

PRESERVATION
WITHOUT
NUTRIENT LOSS

Canning or freezing. With few exceptions, these seem to be our only choices when we want to enjoy ready-to-eat fruits and vegetables out of season. As it is used today, the word "preserves" (like the French word *conserves*) evokes little more than food in cans or jars, preserved through sterilization. However, the original sense of the word was much broader, encompassing all known methods of food preservation.

These days, frozen foods tend to replace canned and bottled goods, since foods lose fewer nutrients through cold than through heat. But freezing is not very satisfactory either: it is expensive, consumes a lot of energy, and destroys many of the vitamins. In the home kitchen, we observe the same development as we have seen in industry: Canning, which was very popular in the 1960s (country folks each with their own sterilizers, putting up their own green beans, shell peas, and tomatoes), has given way to freezing. Emerging relatively recently (sterilization in the nineteenth century, freezing in the twentieth century), these two processes have relegated traditional food-preservation methods to obscurity, if not complete oblivion, as their scope of application has dwindled away. The best example of such displacement is lactic fermentation. Formerly used to preserve all sorts of vegetables, it has survived solely for making sauerkraut, and at that, more for gastronomic reasons than as a preservation process in its own right.

Fortunately, the traditional methods of preservation still live on in the French countryside, although they are rapidly disappearing. There is a wealth of knowledge to be gathered here before it falls into anonymity. That, then, is one of the goals of this book. But far from presenting a study of "preservation ethnology," this collection is meant to be a practical guide. Every recipe we have included is still in use; some have even been enhanced by the advent of new technology, such as high-performance solar dryers and water-sealed lactic-fermentation jars.

STOPPING FOOD CONTAMINATION

Left on its own, most fresh food quickly becomes unfit for consumption. Food is biochemically altered, due to the action of enzymes, and provides microorganisms—primarily bacteria—with a fertile environment in which to grow. To prevent this process, the most radical method is simply to kill the microorganisms by placing the food in an airtight container, and then heating it to temperatures greater than $100°C/212°F$ for a sufficient length of time. This technique, discovered by Nicolas Appert at the beginning of the nineteenth century, gave birth to the canning industry as we know it today.

Other methods of preservation seek to prevent microorganisms from spreading, without necessarily killing them. If the temperature is too low, acidity too high, water content insufficient, or salt concentration too high, microbes simply cannot multiply. As it is equally effective to destroy microorganisms or inhibit their growth, the method chosen should be the one that best protects the appearance, flavor, and nutritional value of the food, without adding undesirable substances. Of course, no method is ideal: During any preservation process, some alteration of the food is unavoidable. Moreover, no one method has proven superior to all others in all cases. And so, for most foods, we have a variety of techniques to choose from, each with its own advantages and disadvantages.

CHOOSING A METHOD OF PRESERVATION

Three methods overwhelmingly dominate the history of food preservation before the industrial age: cellar storage under cool, dark conditions, for certain fruits and winter vegetables (such as root vegetables, tubers, apples, and pears); drying, for fruit; and lactic fermentation for most other vegetables.

Natural-state preservation in a cellar is the most basic way to preserve foods that take well to this method. Although it is possible to dry apples and to lacto-ferment carrots, winter provisioners have traditionally relied on apples stored in a cellar in their natural state, and carrots preserved likewise in a root cellar, or in the ground.

The choice between drying and lactic fermentation is not made arbitrarily. Experience has shown that dried fruits keep much better than most dried vegetables, retaining more flavor and vitamins due to their natural acidity. It is no coincidence that one of the few vegetables traditionally preserved by drying is the tomato, an acidic fruit-vegetable. As for lactic fermentation, people soon discovered that it was an unsuitable method for most fruit: Everyone knows that when fruit is fermented, we get alcoholic beverages.

Applications for the other methods of food preservation described in this book—sugar, salt, oil, vinegar, wine, and alcohol—are more limited, but certainly interesting nonetheless. For example, there are no substitutes for slow evaporation when preserving sugar-free jams, nor for oil or vinegar with herbs, salt with cod, and so on. In practice, the choice is often obvious, and simply depends upon the food to be preserved and its future culinary use.

ALTERING OR ENHANCING?

Inevitably, food is altered in the preservation process. However, unlike sterilization or freezing, many traditional methods do not necessarily result in a loss in flavor or nutritional value. Lactic fermentation, for example, enhances digestion and also increases the enzyme and sometimes the vitamin content, compared with the unfermented food. In other processes, the act of preserving often enhances the flavor of a food rather than its nutritional value. It might seem bizarre to preserve grapes in vinegar when this fruit keeps perfectly well by drying, but any gourmet will tell you that grapes in vinegar are divine with game or poultry.

Preserving basil in oil or vinegar serves two purposes: to preserve the flavor of this precious herb itself, and to impart its flavor to two ingredients used daily in cooking. And while drying preserves fruits, it also increases their sugar content, opening a new world of uses, such as sweetening desserts and certain beverages and providing energy-rich snacks for athletes. In bygone days, North Africans used raisins or dates, not cane sugar, to sweeten tea.

Over fifteen centuries ago, Hippocrates himself pointed out the positive effects of different preservation methods on the quality and properties of meat:

> Meats preserved in wine become dry and are nourishing: they dry out because of the wine; they are nourishing because of the flesh. Preserved in vinegar, they ferment less, because of the vinegar, and are quite nourishing. Meats preserved in salt are less nourishing, as salt deprives them of moisture, but they become lean, dry out, and are sufficiently laxative.[1]

The art of food preservation, which remains in part to be discovered, is this: For each food, use the method that not only best protects its nutritional value, but also enhances its flavor (and occasionally medicinal qualities), according to the eventual use we have in mind.

---

1. Hippocrates, *Du régime*, Edition "Les belles lettres," Paris, 1967.

A NOTE ON FOOD SAFETY

Today, as home gardeners and cooks rediscover the joys of preserving, they often must confront a gap in cultural knowledge. Instead of turning to a parent or grandparent for advice, they turn to government agencies (chiefly the USDA) or to conventional books on canning, which advise sterilizing jars of food in either a boiling water bath or a pressure canner. However, as this book demonstrates, there are many traditional options for putting up fresh food that help food retain more of its flavor and nutritive value.

There is an important distinction to be made between sanitary and sterile conditions. Unless you live in an autoclave or hospital operating room, your kitchen (no matter how sanitary) will be far from sterile. Fortunately, absolute sterility isn't necessary for most aspects of food preservation. For instance, though metal jar lids and tops will need to be boiled and sterilized, you can keep many disease-causing microbes in check simply by washing your hands frequently; by rinsing off raw foods; by thoroughly cleaning all utensils and cutting surfaces; and by following a few commonsense food safety guidelines (such as avoiding "cross-contamination" by using different utensils and surfaces to prepare raw meats and other foods).

In most (though not all) cases, food that has spoiled in storage should be readily apparent. Signs to look for include mold growing inside the lid of the container, on the food itself, or on the outside of the jar. Food that is badly discolored or darkened, or that is smelly or slimy, is likewise suspect and should be thrown away. When food is going bad, small bubbles may form inside a storage jar, and gas or liquid may escape in a rush when you unseal the container.

Remember that the point of preserving food is not to place it forever in suspended animation, but to extend the bounty of the fresh harvest season. Depending upon the type of food and the method of preservation used, this extension, or "shelf life," might range from a few weeks to many months. Think of your pantry or cold cellar as a close cousin to the outdoor cold frame or unheated greenhouse—a simple, low-cost technology that can help you prolong the garden year and make the most of it. Many of the recipes in this book provide estimates on how long the prepared or stored foods will keep in good condition. Using this information, it's possible to enjoy your preserved foods at their peak of flavor, just as you would fresh fruits and vegetables. Here's to good food and good health!

Chapter 1

PRESERVING IN THE GROUND OR IN A ROOT CELLAR

PRESERVING IN THE GROUND OR IN A ROOT CELLAR

NUMEROUS VEGETABLES AND CERtain fruits will keep naturally over the winter season, as long as temperature and humidity are favorably cool and dry, and rodents and other pests are kept away. Natural storage is the easiest method of preservation and grants access all winter to a large selection of fresh vegetables. This method is ideal for those who are lucky enough to have a garden, especially one with well-drained soil, but it is also appropriate for store-bought produce. After all, it is more practical and economical to stock up at harvest time, rather than to run around all winter searching for carrots or apples of good quality.

PRESERVING IN THE GROUND

Some vegetables may remain in the ground all winter, but measures must be taken to protect them, particularly from frost and excess moisture, as well as from rodents (especially in the case of chicory and root vegetables).

Chicory and Escarole

Chicory or escarole, planted

Dried ferns or straw

Two boards of the same length as the planted rows

A few thin wooden strips or some branches

Plastic sheeting (large)

Around November 15, before the severe cold, sink the edges of the boards along the outer length of the planted rows to enclose them. Top with wooden strips or branches, and then with a bed of well-dried ferns or straw. Cover the whole structure with the sheet of plastic, taking care that gutters don't form on the fern layer. At this point, it is also best to trap any slugs. Using this method, chicory or escarole (slightly blanched) will be available right through January, and perhaps later, provided that the cold is not too intense.

Brigitte Lapouge-Degean, Domme

Belgian Endives (Witloof Chicory)

Endive, planted

Soil

On November 1, or before a hard freeze, cut the leaves from the endive, leaving only the crown sticking out of the ground. Cover with at least eight inches of soil.

During the course of the winter, watch for shoots; if there are any, cover them with soil. In March or April, the endive may be unearthed, ready to eat. My garden is at an altitude of approximately 1,640 feet.

Anne-Marie Bouhelier, Clermont-Ferrand

VEGETABLES THAT CAN BE KEPT IN THE GROUND

VEGETABLES	RESISTANCE TO FROST	PRECAUTIONS TO TAKE
Brussels Sprouts Curly Kale	Good	Usually keep all winter. Protect with straw during severe frost.
Cabbage, White or Red Cauliflower	Medium	Can be left in the garden until severe cold.
Carrot	Good	Protect with straw in severe cold.
Chicory Escarole	Limited	Can be preserved in the ground until severe cold hits by protecting with straw. To avoid rotting, remove straw in mild weather. See recipe in this chapter.
Chicory, Wild	Medium	Protect with straw in severe cold.
Endive (root)	Good	See recipe this chapter.
Jerusalem Artichoke	Very good	
Lamb's Lettuce (Mâche)	Good	Usually keeps all winter (small-seed varieties); wait until thaw before picking.
Leek	Good	Usually keeps all winter. Protect with straw during severe frost.
Parsnip	Very good	
Radish, Black	Medium	Protect with straw in severe cold.
Salsify, Black Salsify	Very good	

TRENCHING
(HEELING IN)

This method of preservation allows vegetables to remain planted while protecting them from frost. Cabbage and lettuce are most often preserved this way. From the milder parts of Zone 7 south you can heel them in outdoors, in well-drained soil, but a good cellar is necessary for gardeners in more severe climates.

Cabbage

Cabbage
Soil
Straw or ferns

Dig trenches eight inches deep by eight inches wide, running in an east-west direction. Place the cabbage plants side by side, stems resting on the edge of the trench (south side) and heads resting in the trench. Cover the stems with the soil dug out of the trench. Cover the heads completely with straw or ferns.

Anonymous

Lettuce

Lettuce
Straw matting or branches
and straw

Dig a trench sixteen inches deep and place the lettuce plants in it, roots side by side and not too close to one another. Cover the trench with straw matting or with branches topped with straw.

Anonymous

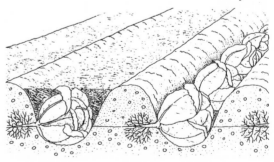

PRESERVING
IN A SILO

Unless one has access to a cool cellar, the silo (as it is commonly known to French gardeners; clamp to an English gardener; the best American synonym is trench) is the best method for preserving root vegetables. Etymologically speaking, the French word *silo* is defined as an "underground excavation used to preserve foods"; however, vegetable silos can be either partially buried or built completely above ground. The most basic silo is simply a hole dug in the ground, or in a mound of well-drained soil or sand. Nevertheless, the following examples show that the possibilities for silo design are endless.

Brick Silo

Vegetables (carrots, turnips, beets, celery, etc.)

2-inch-thick hollow bricks or cement blocks

Wood for the frame and cover

Dried walnut leaves (or other autumn leaves)

Dig a rectangular hole sixteen to thirty-two inches wide by twenty inches deep. Cover the bottom and the walls with bricks. Set the wall bricks on edge; they are secured below by the bottom bricks and above by a wooden frame.

Alternate layers of vegetables with layers of leaves. Finish with a layer of leaves. Close the silo with a heavy, tight-fitting wooden cover to keep out rodents.

Solange and Patrick Cussiez, Aramits

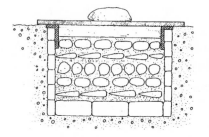

Cabbage Pit Silo

Cabbage
Dried leaves
Plastic sheeting

When the growing season is over and our sauerkraut pot is full, ripe cabbages often remain in the garden but cannot withstand the rigors of winter. To preserve this vegetable, we do the following:

In a dry, well-drained spot that is protected by a hedge or a wall (for example, at the end of a cold frame), dig a 16-inch-deep pit, with its width proportional to the quantity of cabbage to be preserved. Spread the soil and pack it all around the hole, to raise its sides.

Pick the cabbage and remove any leaves that are "too" green, bruised, or rotten. Place the cabbage plants in one layer at the bottom of the hole, roots facing up. Cover the cabbage with autumn leaves that are not too damp. Be careful not to pack them tightly. To protect from the rain, cover with a sheet of plastic or other water-resistant material.

About three to four months later, in early spring, we can once again prepare an excellent sauerkraut.

Beets, carrots, black radishes (with leaves removed), and even geranium plants and cuttings can be kept in the same manner. If different vegetables are to be stored together, they must be arranged such that they can be accessed conveniently without having to dismantle the entire silo. Be sure to reclose it each time.

Bernard Gabard, Péage-de-Roussillon

Semi-Buried Silo

Root vegetables
Sand
Wood ashes
Netting
Plastic or metal sheeting

Dig a hole eight inches deep, and wide enough to accommodate the amount of root vegetables to be preserved. Spread sand and wood ashes to keep out slugs. Place wire mesh hardware cloth at the bottom and around the edges of the hole to stop rodents. (The wire mesh can extend a few inches above the hole). When filling the hole with vegetables, place a small bundle of ½-inch-diameter twigs or tree prunings standing upright in the center to ensure good ventilation.

Spread straw (rye straw, which is long and strong, is ideal) to protect the filled silo from the cold. Use the soil you dug out of the hole to cover the straw. The soil holds the straw in place, increasing airtightness and insulation. Finally, cover the top of the wooden air shaft with a sheet of plastic or metal to protect it from water, and the silo is complete.

When removing vegetables from the silo, open it on the north side to avoid a rise in temperature. I personally make many silos (one for carrots, one for celery, and so on), and obtain very fresh vegetables from them until early June. Even in past years, during rough winters (down to -22°C/-8°F on the ground), my vegetables have never frozen.

Joël Hecquet, Frévent

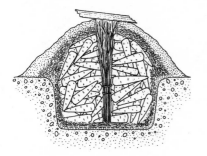

Trench Silo

Root vegetables
Soil
Straw

This method is both simple and effective. Pull the vegetables out of the ground by their leaves, and stack the plants to one side. Dig a trench six inches deep by approximately two feet wide. Place the plants upright in the trench. Cover the entire trench with a 6- to 8-inch-thick dome of topsoil, depending on the severity of your winter conditions. Cover the entire trench with a layer of straw. Vegetables stored in this manner in November will keep fresh; carrots stay very juicy until spring.

Pierre Lochet, Rouziers-de-Touraine

Washer or Steamer Silo

VARIATION 1:

Root vegetables
An old steam-washer, or a
  large steamer
Dried walnut leaves (or
  other autumn leaves)
Straw
A heavy stone
Plastic sheeting

During the winter, the best silo in which to keep root vegetables such as carrots, beets, and turnips, is an old steam-washer (known in French as a *lessiveuse*, a perforated receptacle for washing laundry, different from the washing machines familiar to Americans. A large old vegetable or seafood steamer makes an acceptable substitute). It is usually rustproof and allows the air to circulate through its small

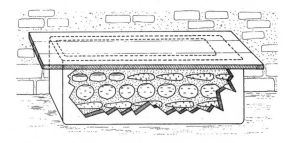

holes. It simply needs to be buried, surrounded on all sides by straw. Put well-dried leaves at the bottom and place the vegetables, with their crowns and root tips removed, on top. Cover successively with a lid, a heavy stone, a layer of straw, and a sheet of plastic. This way, I keep my root vegetables until April or May, even in very rough winter conditions, and I have no waste.

Jacqueline Closset, Belgium

VARIATION 2:

Root vegetables

An old washing-machine drum

Straw or other vegetative insulation

Branches

An old washing-machine drum makes a useful alternative silo. Dig a hole and put the drum in it, leaving the drum's opening slightly above ground. Put root vegetables in the drum, cover them with good dry straw (or with some other vegetative insulating material), and close the drum door. For added protection from animals, we have also used two layers of branches to fence off the silo.

J. and M. Lecoq, Prahecq

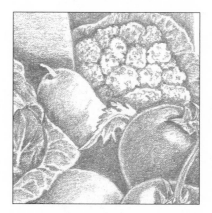

PRESERVING IN
A ROOT CELLAR

The success of this method depends on the quality of the cellar, but more specifically on its temperature, which should remain cool but frostproof right till the end of spring. Under cool, dry conditions, most produce will keep remarkably well, and gardeners in severe climates, where in-ground winter storage is risky, will have a viable option for preserving their harvest.

Apples

✤CAUTION: Apples give off ethylene gas, which makes other produce ripen, sprout, and spoil prematurely, and which can impart an off flavor to cabbage and other vegetables. Be sure to store apples separately from other produce.

Apples
Small crates

Place the apples in small crates, two or three rows high maximum, and store them in a dark cellar that is very cool but protected from frost. It is best to put the crates high off the ground, especially if temperatures are expected to be cold. Identify the contents of the crates (green, ripe, or by type, for example), so that they can be used in the proper order (assuming that you sorted them in the first place). Apples will keep from November to March or longer, depending on the variety. 'Granny Smith', 'Winesap', 'Black Arkansas', 'Idared', and 'Liberty' are some good keepers for American gardeners.

Jean-Yves Cousseau, Millau

Apples in Elderflowers

Apples
Dried elderflowers
Box (preferably wooden)

Pick elderflowers in June, allow them to dry, and store them in an airtight container so that they remain fragrant.

Place a layer of dried elderflowers at the bottom of a box (preferably made of wood). Alternate layers of apples and layers of flowers. Finish with a layer of flowers, and close the box as tightly as possible. Keep in a cool, dry place (provided it is not too damp, a cellar is suitable). After six to eight weeks, the apples may be eaten and will taste like pineapple. This method works especially well for pippins, which can be kept in this way for at least ten weeks. If we place them on a bed of elderflowers in small open crates, they will keep longer, but the pineapple flavor won't be nearly as intense.

A. Motsh, Ambierle

Cabbage

Cabbage
Crates
A tarp

Pick the cabbage before the frost. Remove the roots and the outside leaves, keeping only the firm heads. Handle them gently to avoid bruising. Place the cabbage upside down, in a single layer and not tightly packed, in well-ventilated boxes such as fruit crates.

Stack the crates in a cool, well-ventilated room, and cover them with a tarp. If the room temperature stays low and enough air circulates, the cabbage will keep for several months. From time to time, check the crates, removing any cabbage that is rotting.

M. François, Waziers

Cardoons and Celery

Cardoons or celery
Soil or sand

Cardoons must be brought in to the cellar before the first frost, or else their ribs will burst. They can be preserved until Christmas in a cool place (protected from freezing) by storing them upright with soil covering the roots and watering occasionally. With time, they become even more tender and tasty. Celery will keep in similar fashion, preferably using sand instead of soil.

Annie Dijoud, St. Joseph-de-Rivière

Carrots

VARIATION 1:

Carrots
Crate
Newspaper
Dried walnut leaves (or other autumn leaves)
Small boards, bricks, or blocks

Line a crate with newspaper, and place the carrots upright against one another. Place dried leaves between the rows. Fold the excess newspaper lining back down, and set the crate on the ground, raised up on small boards, bricks, or blocks in a moderately cool cellar.

Marie-Reine Triboulot, Rambervillers

VARIATION 2:

Carrots
Wooden box or plastic barrel
Newspaper

Pick the carrots, clean them, and remove the crowns. Place the carrots in a wooden box or plastic barrel and cover them with newspaper. This way, they keep very fresh for a long time.

J. Devillers, Pont-de-Roide

Chestnuts in Sand

❧ Chestnuts are widely cultivated in France, where they are much sought after for use in soups, stews, side dishes, and desserts. In the United States, you may find these delectable, highly nutritious nuts fresh at the grocery store during the winter. Select heavy, shiny brown ones.

Chestnuts
A can, bucket, or
   large pan
Sand
A screen
A weight

Here is a recipe that I have used for five years to keep chestnuts fresh until Easter. Soak the chestnuts in a large container for two days and remove any that float. Let the chestnuts dry for no longer than one day on a screen situated in a well-ventilated room (out of the sun). There must be no residual water. Fill a can, bucket, or large pan with alternate layers of chestnuts and very dry sand, finishing with a layer of sand. Cover with a screen secured by a weight to keep rodents out. Store the chestnuts in a cool cellar and use them as needed.

I've tried several ways of preserving chestnuts, but this one has given me the most satisfaction. I think the key is soaking them first, but avoid damp sand, or they will soon get moldy.

Chantal Martinet, Vernet-la-Varenne

Chicory and Escarole

Chicory or escarole

Before the frost begins, we pull out chicory and escarole with their roots still attached, and place them tightly together in the cellar to blanch. If they become dry, we moisten the roots. Keeping time is about two months.

Pascale Dey-Marquis, Montigny-en-Gohelle

Endive in Buckets

Endive roots
Buckets
Topsoil
Black plastic

We pull out endive roots and allow them to dry on the ground for a few hours, then remove the leaves just above the crown. We place our roots in buckets along with some topsoil, and store them in the cellar. Whenever we need endive, we bring up a bucket and store it in the kitchen closet, or cover it with black plastic. We water the bucket once or twice, new succulent leaves grow from the roots, and that's how we have endive for part of the winter.

Jean-Yves Cousseau, Millau

Garlic and Onions

Garlic or onions
String

When the garlic or onions are very dry, tie them together in small bunches and hang them upside down in a cool, dry place. 'Yellow Globe', 'White Portugal', and 'Sweet Spanish' onions store well, whereas red onions are short-term keepers. Also, note that hardneck garlic doesn't store as long as softneck (artichoke-type) garlic.

Anne-Marie Bouhelier, Clermont-Ferrand

Leeks

Leeks
Soil or sand

Trim the roots and leaves off the leeks. Replant them tightly together in well-textured soil or sand, and store them in the cellar, watering only once.

Ms. Rosseti and Mr. Mariani, St. Martin-D'Entrannes

Root Vegetables in Barrels or Other Containers

VARIATION I:

Root vegetables
Large barrels, cooking pots, or steamers
Paper or burlap bags
Dried walnut leaves

At harvest time, I cut the crown from root vegetables, so the leaves will not regrow while in storage. Depending on the moisture content, I leave the vegetables to dry for one to several days as necessary; they must not become dehydrated or wilted. I then take my vegetables down to the cellar (safe from freezing), and place them in barrels that are open at one end, or in old cooking pots (even those with a few holes) or old steamers. I use a different container for each type of vegetable I am storing. I then close the containers with their own lids or with several layers of paper (very large bags folded in two). To deter rodents, I close the containers with a burlap bag filled with dried walnut leaves gathered in autumn. Mice seem not to like the smell of walnut leaves.

Depending on the humidity of the room in which the vegetables are stored, the containers will need further opening or closing. If water is condensing on the lid, the container should be opened more, or moisture will be trapped inside and the vegetables will rot. On the other hand, if the vegetables are drying out and wilting, the container should be sealed more tightly to keep the moisture inside. The only way to determine how much to leave the container open is by observation. It is most important to monitor the initial stages of preservation, because vegetables lose most of their water content as they go from a growth phase to a storage phase. Although monitoring may seem quite demanding, it actually happens automatically: When I take out vegetables for use, I check to see whether they are damp or wilting.

Using this method, I keep carrots, beets, radishes, and the like fresh and handy (no need to dig an earth storage trench or cover with sand) until the end of June.

Christine Roger, Switzerland

Variation 2:

Root vegetables
An old steamer or wooden box
Sand

Here is a very easy way to preserve root vegetables, and even chestnuts (we have kept some until March). Simply place your vegetables in big containers (an old steamer or wooden box) and cover them with slightly damp sand. Store in a cool place, such as a cellar or storeroom, but where they will not freeze. You will have fresh vegetables on hand that will keep until spring.

G. and C. Chautemps, Lyon

Root Vegetables in Sand

VARIATION 1:

Root vegetables
Containers
Sand

Root vegetables are buried in sand, which should be neither too dry nor too damp. The sand can be piled on the ground, or kept in boxes or other containers. The containers or pile of sand may be placed in a cool cellar or outdoors in a sheltered location.

Anonymous

VARIATION 2:

Root vegetables
An old refrigerator with no door
Sand
A board large enough to cover refrigerator

In my cellar, I laid down an old refrigerator with its open side facing up, the door removed. At harvest time, just before the real cold starts, I pick healthy roots and leave them in the sun for several hours, so that the soil comes off easily. I cut the leaves about one and a half inches from the base. I then spread a layer of clean sand (not too damp or too dry, to prevent the roots from rotting or shriveling). I arrange a layer of vegetables that are touching but not packed too tightly, and cover them with 1 inch of sand. I repeat this process, alternating layers of vegetables and sand, until the refrigerator is full. I then cover the opening with a board. Roots stacked in this manner will keep from one season to the next. If you decide to stock different vegetables in the same container, it's best to prepare a storage diagram so you know where to find them!

Ghislaine Fayolle, Larajasse

Root Vegetables in Sawdust

✤CAUTION: Lumber often is treated with toxic compounds such as creosote, chromated copper arsenate (CCA), or pentachlorophenol. Therefore, it is essential to ensure that the sawdust you use for food storage comes from untreated wood.

Root vegetables
Containers
Untreated sawdust

Remove crowns and tips of root vegetables. Wash the vegetables thoroughly, then dry and place them in containers filled with sawdust made from untreated wood. Preserved this way, root vegetables keep very well until spring, provided that they are stored in an appropriate place, which is neither too cold (that is, is frostproof) nor too warm.

Anonymous

Tomatoes in Paper

Tomatoes
Paper

Pick green tomatoes at the end of the season and wrap them up individually in paper. Store them in a cool, dark room. Ripen as needed by unwrapping and exposing the tomatoes to warmth and light. They will keep for about three months.

Jean Dey, Montigny-en-Gohelle

PRESERVING AT ROOM TEMPERATURE

This is a popular approach for keeping squash, as well as tomatoes.

Squash in Newspaper

Winter or summer squash
Newspaper

Squash will keep at moderate room temperature, placed well apart on several layers of newspaper. Do not put squash in the cellar (too damp) or the attic (too cold); the best place is right on the kitchen counter. Besides enjoying the decorative qualities of squash, you can monitor their progress. If a squash begins to rot, remove it immediately, before it liquefies completely.

Pascale Dey-Marquis, Montigny-en-Gohelle

SQUASH KEEPING TIMES

VARIETY	AVERAGE PRESERVATION TIME
Zucchini	3 months
Pumpkin, American winter squash, pattypan squash	6 months
Japanese winter squash (also called cabocha, kuri, or Hokkaido squash), turban squash, butternut squash	8 months
Spaghetti squash	8 months

Squash Coated in Oil

Winter or summer squash
A clean rag
Vegetable oil

Before storing, wipe each squash with a clean rag soaked in vegetable oil to avoid the rapid spread of mold. If mold appears, I simply repeat this procedure. Of course, this requires some supervision, but the squash really will keep longer.

Ghislaine Fayolle, Larajasse

Tomatoes

Tomatoes
Newspaper, wrapping paper, or silk

Here's a way to preserve garden tomatoes in their natural state. Uproot tomato plants around the end of September or beginning of October. Wrap each tomato (both ripe and green) in newspaper, or preferably in wrapping paper or silk, and hang the plants by their roots at room temperature (14 to 17°C/57 to 62°F). The fruit keeps well until December or January; the green tomatoes ripen slowly and still seem fresh. This is a proven technique used traditionally in Lorraine with the 'Saint-Pierre' and 'Marmande' varieties.

Dominique and Christiane Stevens-Kintz, Favières

PRESERVING OTHER FOODS IN THEIR NATURAL STATE

Blueberries

Blueberries
Honey
Canning jars and lids
A masher

First, soak the jars in which you will store the berries for twelve hours to allow any mold spores to hatch. Then sterilize the jars in boiling water, just before use.

Sort the blueberries, removing any leaves and bruised berries. Crush the berries with a masher and pour them into the sterilized jars. Fill the jars up to one-half to three-quarters of an inch from the rim. Fill the rest of the way with crushed berries preserved from the previous year. Coat the inside of the lids with honey and close the jars. Blueberries will keep for one year, if stored in the cellar.

In Finland, we eat them with *alkkuna*, which is a cereal made of either rye, barley, or oat flour, combined with pea flour (depending on the region), and roasted. This is really delicious with blueberries added!

Paul Murtomaki, Finland

Whortleberries

Whortleberries
Canning jars
A masher

First, soak the jars in which you will store the berries for twelve hours to allow any mold spores to hatch. Then sterilize the jars in boiling water, just before use.

After picking the berries, sort them, removing the leaves and any spoiled fruit. (In Finland, we use round trays with a bottom that lets leaves and small berries drop through.) Crush the berries with a masher so there is enough juice (it should be foaming) when the purée is bottled. When filling the jars, tap the bottoms to fit in as much pulp as possible. Close the jars and store them in a cellar (10 to 15°C/50 to 60°F). Berries will keep for one to two years.

Some people use them as an accompaniment for game. Hot-cereal lovers mix them in while cooking porridge. Served any way, they are sublime.

Paul Murtomaki, Finland

Olives

❧ Although Americans find olives growing only in southern California, this staple of Mediterranean cooking sometimes appears fresh at specialty markets in the United States.

Fresh black olives
Herbs
Olive oil
Canning jars

Pick black olives in December, keeping only the ones that are good. Scald jars, dry them, fill them with olives and seal them airtight. Store until March in the cellar, the attic, or a dark closet. Then the olives will be ready to eat. They'll have lost their black color and become greenish, but once the jar is opened, they'll blacken again and remain slightly bitter.

Season these olives with herbs (thyme and marjoram, for example), salt and pepper, and sprinkle with olive oil. At this stage, they'll keep for only a few days.

Occasionally, olives stored in a jar will mold. If they do, open the jar, rinse the olives, and season them as just described. If this happens before March (when we usually eat them), they will be more bitter, but are still just as good.

With this recipe, we can preserve olives with their full flavor for at least six months. Once traditionally used in Provence, this method is now used less and less.

J. Barallier, Auriol

Gruyère Cheese in Ashes

Gruyère cheese
Sifted wood ashes
A stoneware pot

Take a piece of Gruyère that is not too thin. Put it in a stoneware pot and surround the cheese with one to one and a half inches of sifted wood ashes. Store the pot in the cellar. Three months later, the cheese will be as fresh as when it was stored.

Jean Roger, Jully

Clarified Animal Fat

4½ lbs. beef fat
2+ lbs. pork fat
Onions
Leeks
Carrots
Turnips
A bouquet garni (parsley, thyme, and other herbs, tied in a small bundle)
Salt
Horseradish
A large, cast-iron pot
Cheesecloth
An earthenware pot

To reconnect with the past and preserve fat in the good old style of Normandy, finely cut up four and a half pounds of beef fat and a bit more than two pounds of pork fat. Put it all in a large cast-iron pot with onions, leeks, carrots, turnips, a bouquet garni, salt, horseradish, and any other seasonings you may like. Simmer over very low heat for several hours until the fat liquefies. Filter this liquid through a piece of cheesecloth to obtain very clear fat. The clarified fat will keep for several years if stored in an earthenware pot and kept in a cool place. It makes a good substitute for commercial meat concentrates when preparing broth.

Sylvie Bercon, Mayenne

Clarified Butter (Ghee)

Unsalted butter
A large, thick-bottomed pot
A skimmer
A terrine with a tight lid
Aromatic herbs (optional)

If you have an excess amount of butter, use the Indian method of preservation, that is, convert it into ghee (clarified butter). In a large, thick-bottomed pot, melt two to eleven pounds of unsalted butter on very low heat. Do not stir. It must cook for at least five to six hours to allow the water to evaporate and the solids to rise to the surface. From time to time, skim the solids off the top. Watch that the ghee does not burn, or it will turn brown. When done, it should be amber colored and crystal clear. At this point, pour the ghee slowly into a terrine, allow it to solidify, and then store it, tightly closed, in a cool place. Ghee will keep for months, even unrefrigerated.

You can add aromatic herbs to the ghee during cooking. Clarified butter is used for sauces and frying.

Sylvie Bercon, Mayenne

❧ Chapter 2 ❧
PRESERVING
BY DRYING

ꙫ *Chapter 2* ꙫ

PRESERVING
BY DRYING

THE MOST ANCIENT FOOD PRESERVA-
tion method, drying remains widely
in use today. Its popularity in hot, dry
climates is easily understood; however, by
employing solar dryers or other types of
heaters, we can also dry food in cool, damp
climates.

Whereas we have always dried fruits,
why is it that vegetables are much less commonly dried, and then only a few types, at
that?

Several explanations can be given:

1. Many vegetables lose a good deal of
their flavor when dried, which is not the
case with fruits.

2. Drying depletes much more of the
vitamin content in vegetables (except for
tomatoes) than in fruits; in effect, the acidity
of fruits preserves vitamins better.

3. Lactic fermentation is a better technique for vegetables; it does not alter flavor
and better retains vitamin content.

While they surely were unaware of vitamins, through intuition and experience our ancestors discovered that drying is suitable for only a few types of vegetables. On the other hand, it is perfectly effective for most fruits, mushrooms, certain herbs, and fish.

GENERAL DRYING METHODS AND MATERIALS

Food usually is dried on a flat surface, such as a tray or screen, using a natural or artificial heat source. Solar drying is obviously the preferred method because it consumes only the sun's energy and that energy is free. Trays should be placed in a dry, well-ventilated spot, generally out of the direct sun, or in specially designed solar dryers.

In lieu of natural sunshine, we can take advantage of the heat generated by a radiator, kitchen range, woodstove, or oven. If all these are lacking, we can settle for a low-wattage electric food dehydrator. Several models are available for home use.

Two Types of Easy-to-Make Drying Trays

Variation 1:
Screened Drying Tray (60" × 20")

Square battens (cross-section 1¼" × 1¼")

Flat battens (cross section ⅛" × 1¼")

20"-wide roll of galvanized metal or rigid plastic screen with fine mesh (25–50 mm or 1–2 sq. in.)

Nails (2" and 1" long)

First assemble the square battens to form a frame sixty inches long by twenty inches wide. To make the frame more rigid, add one or two square battens across the middle. Hammer the frame together with 2-inch nails.

Unroll the screening and flatten it against the frame using the flat battens to hold it in place. Fasten with 1-inch nails. This creates the bottom of the tray.

The tray is now ready to use. Note that the trays can be stacked to save space.

Henry Rouy, Cournon-D'Auvergne

VARIATION 2: SMALL MULTIPURPOSE DRYER
(for those with limited space)

Two 24" × 2½" boards
Two 14" × 2½" boards
Small wooden laths
   (strips)
Small nails

This is a basket that can be hung from a beam or a nail, in the cellar or kitchen. It is very simple to make.

Make the sides of the basket with the four boards. Then nail the small wooden laths three-quarters of an inch apart to make the bottom.

To make the handle, add two small boards of the same length as the basket to each side. Connect them with a round stick.

You can dry cheese, mushrooms, prunes, and herbs for infusions, for example, by placing some netting over the bottom of the basket. This small dryer is easy to move and clean.

Nicole Mansard, St. Julien-Chapteuil

DRYING FRUITS

American Mountain Ash Berries

American mountain ash
   berries
A jar

The mountain ash tree yields berries that delight birds, but often are overlooked by people. Nevertheless, this fruit is one of the richest in vitamin C.

It is best to pick ash berries after the first frost, when they become somewhat less acidic. Let them dry in bunches in a dry, well-ventilated area. Once dry, remove the berries and put them into a jar. This way, you can have them on hand anytime, either whole or powdered for mixing into hot cereals or beverages.

Louis Daumas, Manosque

Apples in an Electric Dehydrator

Apples
An electric dehydrator
Glass jars
Cloth bags

Cut the apples into thin slices, leaving the skin on but removing the seeds. To prevent the apples from turning brown while they are drying, soak the slices in water and lemon juice before placing them in the dryer. This method also minimizes the loss of Vitamin C. Place the fruit on the drying trays. The apples will dry in approximately three hours; they should break easily, since the slices are thin. Store them in glass jars.

I serve these apples as an appetizer, or give them to the kids as snacks, along with a few roasted hazelnuts and almonds.

If the slices are somewhat thicker, they will be softer than the thin slices after about three hours of drying, so they are better kept in cloth bags. I use them for baking fruit cakes, or in *clafoutis* (a dessert similar to a cobbler, baked in a dish with fruit on the bottom and batter on the top. Black cherries traditionally are used in the Limousin region, where this dessert originated). The liquid in the batter softens the apple slices, and the clafoutis tastes as good as with fresh apples.

Nathalie Demarest, Mayenne
Eva Wiehl, Buis-les-Barronies

Apples Dried in the Oven

Apples
Oven
Tin cans or jars

VARIATION 1:

Choose sweet apples. Peel, core, and soak them in cold salted water. Slice them into ¼-inch-thick rounds, and wipe them dry before placing on racks. Put them in a 60°C/140°F oven for three hours on three or four consecutive days, turning them over each time. When they are dry, the rounds should be hard; leave them out in a dry place one or two more days. You can also dry apples by putting them in a bread oven for four hours, after having baked bread. Store them in tin cans to protect from moisture.

Eric and Sylvie Courtille, Lacapelle-Marival

VARIATION 2:

Parboil the apples for two minutes and cut them into thin slices. Put them in an oven just used to bake bread once the oven temperature has dropped to 40 to 45°C/105 to 115°F. Test dryness with the tip of a knife, and allow apples to cool completely (to avoid condensation) before sealing them in airtight jars or tin (not aluminum) cans. Dried this way, apples keep for several months.

G. Petrelli, Pontailler-sur-Soane

VARIATION 3 (IN A WOOD-FIRED COOKSTOVE):

With a few stitches, attach a cloth to the oven rack and lay out the fruit slices, very close together. Leave the oven door slightly ajar with a wooden spoon (my grandmother used to do it this way!).

G. Petrelli, Pontailler-sur-Soane

Apple Paste (Sugar-Free)

Apples
A bowl
A strainer
A food mill
A large pan
Trays or fine screens
   covered with cloth
Drying apparatus

This recipe is suitable for apples that have fallen off the tree (particularly 'Court-pendu', 'Belle-fleur', and various pippin varieties).

Wash the fruit and remove any damaged parts, but otherwise keep the skin on and the seeds intact. Steam the apples for forty minutes (or cook for fifteen minutes in a pressure cooker). After cooking, let the apples drain overnight into a bowl. (Collect the juice to make a clear jelly by adding the same amount of sugar, and boiling the mixture for two minutes).

Pass the well-drained apples through a food mill set on "fine." Dry out the purée as much as possible in a large pan, over low heat. Stir constantly until the paste comes easily off your spoon.

Spread the paste in ½-inch layers on trays or fine screens that have been covered with a cotton or linen cloth, such as cheesecloth (the cloth will end up badly stained but can be used again). Let the paste dry in a food dryer for about twenty hours. The paste will reduce to a thin brown-colored sheet. It peels easily off the cloth and can be cut with scissors. Eat it as is, or rehydrate it.

Pascale Dey-Marquis, Montigny-en-Gohelle

String-Dried Apples

VARIATION 1:

Apples
A peeler and corer
Butcher's string
Radiator
A clean cloth
Plastic or cloth bags, or tin cans

Peel whole apples at the end of winter, when they begin to wrinkle. Core and slice them into ¼-inch rounds. Thread the rounds onto sturdy string (such as butcher's string), and shape the strings into ½-pound necklaces, which are to be hung above one or more radiators. If the radiator is located under a window, several necklaces can be hung from the window hardware. If the radiator is only lukewarm, you can start the drying process by placing the necklaces on a clean cloth set directly on it. Depending on the radiator temperature, it can take anywhere from four to six days for the fruit to dry. At the end of the drying process the rounds will have shrunk by half, but will feel flexible. It is best to start tasting them after the fourth day. Store them in plastic bags that you've sealed after letting out all the air; put them away or hang them in a dry, cool place. The apples will keep for one year. Tin cans or cloth bags certainly would be equally suitable.

Ruth Goldstein, Canteleu

VARIATION 2: APPLES DRIED WITH ELDERFLOWERS

Pippin-type apples
A peeler and corer
String
Stove or boiler
Tin can or wooden box
A handful of dried elderflowers (from the previous summer)

Core the apples and slice them into ¼-inch rounds. Thread them on a string, through the center hole, and dry them over the stove or a central heating boiler until they become flexible. Seal them in a tin can or a wooden box, along with a handful of dried elderflowers. The apples will take on a delicious taste of pineapple, and keep indefinitely.

Pascale Dey-Marquis, Montigny-en-Gohelle
Andrée Motsh, Amierle

Apricots

Ripe apricots
Drying apparatus

Choose apricots that are very ripe. Cut in half, pit them, and place them on dryer trays, cut side up. Turn the apricots over occasionally.

Anonymous

Bananas

Bananas
Drying apparatus
Bags

You've bought too many bananas, and they're starting to blacken. Peel them and let them dry—whole or cut in half lengthwise—on a screen or tray in a dry, well-ventilated place. A few days later, the bananas will be ready to eat and will keep for quite some time in closed bags. Delicious, energizing, and easy to take along, they make excellent snacks for kids. Preserved this way, they are more nutritious than commercially dried bananas, which are usually sterilized and coated in sugar!

Babette Cezza, Vergt

Black Currants

Black currants
Drying apparatus; trays
  need fine mesh

Dry whole currants on trays covered with fine mesh (the type used for bug netting).

Jean Roger, Jully

Blueberries

Blueberries

Drying apparatus; trays
   need fine mesh

Blueberries lend themselves well to drying. Sort them carefully, removing leaves and twigs, and leave them to dry slowly on a tray covered with fine mesh. Blueberries can stay out overnight, as their skin is fully intact and protects them from moisture. They dry within a week. The yield is somewhat small, but the taste is excellent.

Marc Hollenstein, La Bastide-de-Juvinas

Blueberry Paste

Blueberries

A saucepan

Honey

A greased baking sheet

Cook the blueberries without water over low heat, stirring constantly, until they turn into a thick compote. Add honey, to taste.

    Spread the compote over a greased baking sheet, and with the oven door ajar, let it dry on low heat. When dry, this paste will keep for several months in an airtight tin can.

Anonymous

Cherries

Cherries

Drying apparatus

Pit the cherries and place them on drying trays. While pitting is time-consuming, cherries prepared this way don't have the bitter aftertaste found in dried unpitted cherries gathered off the ground in August. Cherries dry in three to four days if left outside overnight. (Night dew dries after one-half hour of morning sun, during which time the cherries will brown, but will retain their original taste.)

Marc Hollenstein, La-Bastide-de-Juvinas

Chestnuts

Chestnuts
A bucket
Vinegar
Small crates

Soak the chestnuts for forty-eight hours in a bucket of water with a few drops of vinegar added. Rinse, and repeat twice more (this makes three times in all, for a total of six days of soaking). Each time, remove any chestnuts that float, as these may contain worms. Arrange the remaining chestnuts in a single layer in small crates, and put them out to dry in the sun. Bring them in at night to avoid dew. Drying takes about one week; then store the chestnuts in a dry room.

This method makes it possible to preserve chestnuts until April or May. They will continue to harden and must be rehydrated, but will retain their full flavor. This is an old recipe from Allevard, in the Dauphiné region of the French Alps.

Annie Dijoud, St. Joseph-de-Rivière

Chestnuts (Peeled)

Chestnuts
Oil
Drying apparatus
Canvas bags

Peel off both skins of the chestnuts. The first one comes off easily, but the second one comes off only after soaking in boiling water. An even more effective method is to soak the chestnuts in boiling oil. The second skin, now all dried up, will then peel off easily. (Be careful! Use rags or wear gloves so you don't burn your hands.) Let the chestnuts dry on wicker trays, either in a dehydrator or in the kitchen at room temperature. Once dry, store them in canvas bags (they will mold in glass jars). After soaking, I cook them to make chestnut purée.

Colette Gilbert, Neuilly-Plaisance

Figs

Figs
Fig leaves
Thorny branches

To help them dry, dip the figs for three seconds in boiling water to which you've added two fig leaves.

Let the figs dry exposed to the air and in the sun. To do this, take any kind of thorny branches twelve to sixteen inches long, and hang them from a horizontal beam with their thorns pointing up. Pin the figs to the thorns.

Catherine Taisne, Calcatoggio

Fruit Paste (Sugar-Free)

Fruit
A large, flat baking dish

Cook the fruit with very little or no added water at all (depending on how moist the raw fruit is), and then crush it to make a very thick compote.

Spread a ½-inch-thick (maximum) layer in a large, flat baking dish. Leave the compote to dry for forty-eight hours or longer, on low heat such as from a wood-fired oven, or from a gas stove set at 60°C/140°F. The compote will dry and turn into a fruit paste. Cut it into squares or rectangles, and store it in tightly closed containers.

Jacqueline Maitte-Lobbe, L'Hermenault

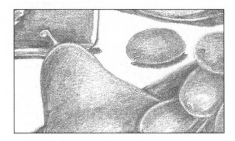

Grapes

VARIATION 1:

Grapes (in bunches)

A few years ago, I discovered this recipe by chance. (This is in fact a rediscovery. This ancient method is traditionally used in most Mediterranean countries.) That particular year, grapes were plentiful in the Beaujolais vineyards. Grape tarts, grape jams, grape juice . . . all these frequently appeared at my table! But some bunches of grapes looked so beautiful that I didn't want to eat them. I hung them from a beam in my dining room as decoration. Much to my surprise, they kept well, dried gradually, and we ate them as raisins that Christmas!

I've successfully repeated this experience in the years since then. A few small pointers: Pick ripe grapes in the morning, after the dew has dried (moisture will impede preservation considerably). The bunches must be gathered very carefully. Cut them with pruning shears or a pruning knife, including a 4- to 6-inch-long stem, which seems to enhance preservation.

Hang the bunches from the ceiling of a not-too-bright room that has little or no heat (but has a constant temperature). Check frequently, and remove any grapes that are damaged or questionable, without bruising the others. Do not wait later than January to eat the dried grapes.

Ghislaine Fayolle, Larajasse

VARIATION 2:

Grapes

Drying apparatus

The 'Perlette' ('Thompson's Seedless' in North America) variety, quite early and seedless, makes excellent raisins. You can simply dry them by the bunch, but the drying will go faster if you remove the grapes first. Set out the grapes in a greenhouse, or even better, in a solar food dryer. Drying takes awhile (at least one week in a dryer). Protect well from wasps.

Christiane Barroux, Damazan

Peaches

Peaches

Drying apparatus

Pit the peaches, cut them into quarters, and place them on dryer trays. Turn them over several times daily.

Yves Jury and Marie Poscia, Hyères
Jean Roger, Jully

Pears

Pears
Drying apparatus
Cloth bags

VARIATION 1:

Cut ripe pears in half, cover them with a cloth, and place them in the sun for five or six consecutive days. If necessary, complete the drying process in an open oven. Using this method, we've dried juicy 'William's' pears, which we've preserved for several months with no problem.

Hélène and Sylvain Jaworski, Fay-de-Bretagne

VARIATION 2:

Choose pears that are perfectly ripe, but not overripe. With a knife, remove the pits by hollowing out the pears from the bottom end. Cut the fruit lengthwise into two, three, or four sections, depending on the size of the pears. Set them out in the sun; they will dry in three to five days and become delicious.

Marc Hollenstein, La-Bastide-de-Juvinas

VARIATION 3:

Varieties of pears meant for cooking usually need to be cooked before they taste good. But there is a very simple technique that resolves both the taste and preservation problems, as follows: Just cut the pears into quarters, put them on a screen (skin side down), and dry in a woodstove. The quarters shrink rapidly and are ready to eat after two days of drying. You could also dry them in an electric oven with the door left open (oven temperature should be lower than 50°C/125°F), but that would consume a lot of electricity.

Pears preserved this way are delicious, and will keep very well in a cloth bag hanging in a dry, well-ventilated room.

Marie-Reine Triboulot, Rambervillers

Persimmon

Persimmons
Drying apparatus

Using a sharp knife, cut the persimmons into ¼-inch slices. The fruit should be firm yet as ripe as possible. (Picking them as they ripen is the best way to ensure this.) Turn the slices over before they thoroughly dry, or they may stick to the tray. The tart or bitter taste of persimmon completely disappears with drying.

Eva Wiehl, Buis-les-Baronnies

Plums

VARIATION 1:

Plums
Drying apparatus

Cut the plums in half, remove the pits, and spread the fruit, cut side up, in a greenhouse, out in the sun (protected from insects), or in a solar food dryer.

Christiane Barroux, Damazan

VARIATION 2 (FOR DARK PLUMS):

Plums
Small crate
A pane of glass

Place whole plums in a small, well-ventilated crate, covered with a pane of glass. Keep the crate in the sun (ideally, against a wall facing due south). Finish drying in the oven.

Annie Dijoud, St. Joseph-de-Rivière

VARIATION 3:

Plums
A cooking pot
1 tablespoon olive oil
1 tablespoon wood ashes
    in a sachet
5 or 6 peach leaves
    (optional)
A metal strainer
Drying apparatus

Fill a pot with water and add the oil, the ashes, and the peach leaves. Bring this to a boil. Scald the plums by pouring the boiled mixture over them in a metal strainer for three to four seconds. Let them dry on a fine screen, directly in the sun, or in a solar food dryer. When the plums are dry, wash them in clear water, and put them in an oven that has been turned off, but is still warm.

Catherine Taisne, Calcatoggio

Raspberries and Red Currants

Raspberries or red
  currants
Drying apparatus; trays
  need fine mesh

Dry the berries whole on screens outfitted with fine mesh.

Jean Roger, Jully

Strawberries

Strawberries
Drying apparatus

Cut the strawberries in half and dry them, cut side up, in a solar dryer.

Christiane Barroux, Damazan

DRYING VEGETABLES

Sun-Dried Artichokes

Artichokes
A cooking pot
Juice of two lemons
A bouquet garni (basil,
  celery leaves, and so
  on)
Drying apparatus
Paper bags or glass jars

Clean the artichokes and remove any hard leaves. Cut off the sharp tips, as well as the bottoms if they are too hard and stringy. Cut each artichoke into four to six pieces.

Bring a pot of water to a boil along with the juice of two lemons and the bouquet garni. When it boils, toss in the artichokes and cook them al dente. Drain and place on a tray in the sun. When all the cooking water has evaporated from the artichokes, move them to the shade to dry. (If you're using a solar dryer, cover it with a cloth.)

Dried artichokes keep very well in paper bags or in jars. Before cooking them, soften in very hot water.

Anonymous

Cardoons

Cardoons
Drying apparatus

After removing the strings and the surrounding membrane from the cardoon ribs, cut them into 2-inch-long by ¾-inch-thick sticks. Soak them in boiling water for three minutes, and dry with a cloth. Place one layer on each drying tray.

Odile Angeard, Cognin

String-Dried Eggplant

Eggplant
Coarse salt
String
Jars or boxes

Slice the eggplant in rounds, and cover them with coarse salt for several hours to draw out the liquid. Drying should be done on a string; avoid using a wire, as it may rust. Place out of direct sun. Dried eggplant will keep in jars or in tightly closed boxes, if protected from moisture, air, and vermin.

To rehydrate, all you have to do is soak the eggplant for a few hours ahead of time.

P. and K. Bercon-Mene, Mayenne

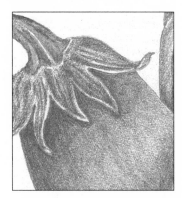

String-Dried Green Beans

Green beans
Salted water
A cooking pot
Butcher's string
Sewing needle
Paper bags

Choose a dry time of the year for this old method of preservation, which requires minimum use of energy. It is known in America as "leather breeches," and is especially suitable for long, skinny snap pole beans.

Remove the strings from the beans. Blanch the beans for two minutes in salted water and drain. Then take thin string (such as butcher's string) and use a sewing needle to string the beans in garlands. Hang these garlands in a dark, dry, well-ventilated place.

Once dry (in about one to two weeks), store the beans in paper bags. Soak them overnight before cooking; one dry ounce per person is enough.

Susanne Förtsch, Malemort

Onions

Onions
Drying apparatus
Canvas bags

In spring, onions tend to rot quickly, so I peel them, slice them in rounds, and place them in a dehydrator. When the onions are dry, I store them in canvas bags and add them to soups just as they are, or to grains as they cook, or to other vegetables.

Irène Clua, Durban-Corbières

Spinach, Orach, or Beet Leaves

Greens
Drying apparatus
Paper bags or tin cans

Use a low-energy electric food dryer. Dry the fresh, clean leaves without washing them first. Place in thin layers on the drying trays, and remove the leaves when they break easily. Store in large paper bags or in tin cans without folding the leaves. When using greens, allow one dry ounce per person, cooked in one and a half quarts of boiling water.

Beet ribs should be removed and dried separately. Cut them into 2-inch-long by ¼-inch-thick sticks. It is best to dip them in boiling water for a few seconds before drying them.

Odile Angeard, Cognin

Sweet Peppers

Sweet peppers
Drying apparatus

Cut the peppers into 1-inch strips and let them dry slowly. They keep very well, and give a nice flavor to soups.

Mrs. Hery, Anduze

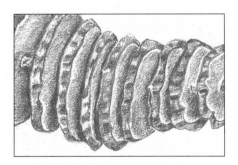

Tomatoes Dried Naturally

Tomatoes
Almond oil (or another
    mild oil)
A clean rag
Drying apparatus
A glass jar

Tomatoes are by far the vegetable most often preserved by drying in various forms.

We prefer to use the 'Beefsteak' variety, a pulpy tomato with fewer seeds.

Peel the tomatoes. (If this poses a problem, soak them for a few seconds in boiling water.) Cut them lengthwise (from bottom to top) into slices approximately ¼-inch thick and remove the seeds. Place the slices on a clean rag to absorb the juice. Oil the dryer screen lightly, preferably with mild almond oil, so that the slices will not stick. When the slices are dry on one side, turn them over; they will be hard when dry. Store the tomatoes well packed in a glass jar.

To use, pour one cup of boiling water over one-half to three-quarter ounces of dried tomatoes per person, and leave them to soften for a few minutes. Add a teaspoon of olive oil, season to your taste, and serve with a purée or a grain dish. We also add these tomatoes to grains or vegetables that are nearly done cooking.

Odile Angeard, Cognin

Stuffed Dried Tomatoes in Oil

Tomatoes
Parsley
Garlic
Anchovy fillets (optional)
Fresh basil leaves
    (optional)
Oil
Drying apparatus
A glass jar

I dry my tomatoes in a solar dryer, cut in half and seeded (easily done with a small spoon). When the tomatoes are dry, stuff a little finely chopped parsley and garlic between the two halves. If you like, add an anchovy fillet, or a basil leaf. Place the reassembled tomatoes in a jar and cover with oil. These are delicious added to a salad during winter.

Anonymous

Sun-Dried Tomatoes in Oil

VARIATION 1:

4 lbs. tomatoes
1 lb. coarse salt
Oil
Drying apparatus
Gauze
A clean, dry cloth
Glass jars

Choose very ripe, small, oblong tomatoes. The Italian variety 'Principe Borghese' is an excellent drier, as are many smaller plum or "paste" tomatoes.

Cut the tomatoes in half, place them on a tray set in the sun, add salt, and cover with gauze to protect from insects. During the day, turn the tomatoes over twice; at night, bring them inside to protect from moisture.

A few days later, when you see that they are very dry but not totally dehydrated, remove some of the salt with a clean, dry cloth. Put the tomatoes into jars and cover them with approximately three-quarters of an inch of oil over the tomatoes, coming up to three-eighths of an inch below the rim. Close the jars tightly and store them in a cool place. In Italy, tomatoes preseved in this manner are eaten as hors d'oeuvres, with no additional preparation.

Marie-Christine Martinot-Aronica, St. Dizier

VARIATION 2:

Tomatoes
Vinegar
Hot peppers, mint leaves,
   or whole garlic cloves
   (optional)
Oil
Drying apparatus
A glass jar

Choose tomatoes that are firm and completely intact, preferably plum tomatoes. Cut them in half lengthwise. Allow them to dry on trays in the sun, bringing them in whenever it is humid, and in at night to avoid dampness. When they are dry, soak the tomatoes in warm vinegar for twenty minutes. Drain and put them in a jar, alternating layers of tomatoes with one or two hot peppers, mint leaves, or whole cloves of garlic. Press well to allow any air to escape, and then cover with oil. These tomatoes will keep for a very long time. We eat them as hors d'oeuvres or with rice, pasta, meat, or fish.

Babette Cezza, Vergt

Sun-Dried and Fermented Tomato Coulis

Tomatoes
Salt
Olive oil
A stoneware or
    earthenware jar
A wooden spatula
A strainer
A bowl
A masher
A cloth bag
Small glass jars
Waxed paper

Put very ripe tomatoes, cut in half but with seeds and all, into a stoneware or earthenware jar. Leave to ferment for eight days, taking care to stir daily with a wooden spatula. When the eight days are up, strain the contents into a bowl. Crush the tomatoes carefully with a masher, and pour the sauce obtained into a cloth bag to remove all the liquid. Hang the bag and let it drain for two days.

Spread the coulis on a plate and leave it out in the sun to dry for several days. Add salt to taste and stir with a wooden spatula. Fill small jars with the coulis and cover with olive oil. Close the jars with waxed paper (or lids).

J. Barallier, Auriol

String-Dried Turnips

Turnips
Cotton thread or kitchen
    string
A pie tin or cookie sheet
An airtight box

Clean the turnips (skin can be left on), and cut into ⅛-inch-thick slices. String them on cotton thread or on kitchen string, leaving space between the slices. Hang the strings up in a dry place (attic, kitchen), and let the turnips dry. It may take one or two weeks, depending on the room and its level of humidity.

Once they are very dry, unstring the turnips and put them in a single layer on a pie tin or a cookie sheet. Place that in the oven at a low temperature (60°C/140°F) for five minutes. Cool completely and store the tunrips in an airtight box. I have kept some for five years.

Dried turnips are perfect for a nice vegetable broth, to which they add color, and for beef stew.

Denise Pesleux, Ceret

Vegetable Bouillon Powder

Celeriac, celery leaves,
    carrots, garlic, leeks,
    onions
Brewer's yeast
Olive oil
Tomatoes (optional)
Parsley, basil, and other
    herbs (optional)
Drying apparatus
Blender
Small glass jars

Dry the celeriac, celery leaves, carrots, garlic, leeks, and some onion. Once dry, place these vegetables in a blender, reduce to a powder, and combine with brewer's yeast and olive oil. The powder will keep one to two years stored in small jars in a dry place.

You can vary the ingredients, for example, to make a bouillon cube with dried sliced tomatoes (put through the blender) as the predominant flavor.

These mixtures, high in mineral salts, are especially convenient for vegetarians who don't use meat broth and who don't want a lot of salt in their cooking. This vegetable mix can also be used to season soups or grain dishes.

You can also dry parsley, basil, celery leaves, and other aromatic herbs, which will keep their color and flavor for one year if stored in airtight jars. Reduce them to a powder and blend them into mixes as I've explained, or better yet, keep them in separate small jars to have them on hand for specific flavorings and uses.

Eva Wiehl, Buis-les-Baronnies

Wild Vegetables

Nettle, plantain, wild
  spinach
Drying apparatus
Cloth bags

In early spring (on a "leaves" day, according to Maria Thun's Biodynamic calendar, which shows the best time to sow, plant, and harvest according to the moon's position within the constellations), we gather nettle, plantain, and wild spinach. We dry them in the shade, and store them in cloth bags for soups in the wintertime. A trick for nettle and wild spinach is to cut the plants down to the ground after harvesting, and they will grow back. This way, we can use these precious friends until the fall.

Andrée and Maurice Leroy, Abries-en-Queyras

String-Dried Zucchini

Zucchini
String
Thin cloth
A cloth bag

Slice zucchini into ¼-inch rounds and thread these on strings about twenty inches long. Hang the strings out in the sun, well exposed. Cover them with a thin cloth to protect from flies. Let the zucchini dry for a few days, then store it in a cloth bag.

Lise Colomb, Lablachère

DRYING HERBS AND FLOWERS

A few guidelines:

✤ Pick plants in the morning, when it is dry and sunny and they are at their peak, depending on the plant and the part that you are using.

✤ Wash plants only when necessary (roots, for example).

✤ Always dry plants in the shade (outdoors) or in a dark place (indoors).

✤ Drying is complete when plants are dry and brittle.

✤ Store dried plants in glass jars, paper, or cardboard boxes, away from light. Plants can also be hung in a dry, well-ventilated place.

✤ Label the containers you use to hold plants.

✤ With every new harvest, discard plants left over from the previous year.

Farigoulade *(Thyme Medley)*

1 heaping teaspoon thyme
½ teaspoon savory
½ teaspoon oregano
1 heaping teaspoon thyme
A coffee mill

Pick these plants just as they are starting to flower, and allow them to dry in the dark. Remove any very woody parts, and grind the herbs to a fine powder using a coffee mill.

Serve this medley with grilled mutton. We place a spoonful in one corner of our plates and dip pieces of meat into it. It's a gourmet's delight!

Anne-Marie Arrouye, Aix-en-Provence

Herbs in Bags

Herbs with long stems (rosemary, basil, tarragon, sage, mint, etc.)

Paper bags

This method works well for long-stemmed herbs, such as rosemary, basil, tarragon, sage, and mint. Place the heads of the herbs (separated by type) all the way inside a paper bag; gather the stems together, and tie them up along with the open end of the bag. Make holes in the bag for ventilation, and hang it in a not too cool, not too warm, well-ventilated, and preferably dark place. (Herbs lose their flavor when exposed to light.)

Ghislaine Fayolle, Larajasse

Herbs in Open-Air Bouquets

Herbs (parsley, sage, thyme, bay leaves, tarragon, mint, marjoram)

Glass jars

This is a particularly effective technique for parsley, sage, thyme, bay leaves, tarragon, mint, and marjoram. Make little bouquets of herbs (separated by type), and hang them in a dry, well-ventilated place, preferably in the dark. When the herbs are dry, the leaves can be separated from the stems, and stored in airtight glass jars.

M. Buisson, Riorges

Herbs on Trays

Herbs

Small cloth-lined crates, or trays made with screening or muslin

Place a shallow layer of plants in small crates, lined at the bottom with cloth, or on trays made with screening or muslin. Small crates, or trays with "feet," can be stacked. Put the crates or trays in a dark, dry, well-ventilated place (such as the attic).

Jeannette Roy, Vergigny

Linden Flowers

Linden flowers
2 clean dishtowels
Tin cans or glass jars

Follow the same procedure as for rose petals (below). This way, each room will have a different scent.

You can also make a mild, soothing tea from dried linden flowers, which are highly prized in France for this purpose. The American basswood tree, widespread throughout the eastern United States, is in the linden family and produces suitable flowers.

Rose Petals

Rose petals
2 clean dishtowels
Tin cans or glass jars

To dry rose petals properly, they must be spread out in thin layers and protected from light and dust. So, on a clean dishtowel, which I've placed on the top of a cabinet, I spread the freshly gathered rose petals, and cover them with another dishtowel. While drying, they give the room an exquisite scent! After several weeks, I store them in tin cans or glass jars labeled with the plant's name and the harvest year.

Lise Marie Ratier, La Ferrière

Summer Scents

Mixed herbs (thyme, bay leaves, rosemary, wild thyme, savory, etc.)
3 cloves
½ teaspoon grated nutmeg
Small piece of dried chili (optional)
A salad bowl
A glass jar

Gather a bouquet of mixed herbs. Set them out to dry right away in a dark, dry place. Remove the leaves from herbs with hard stems (thyme and rosemary, for example). Combine two tablespoons of each herb with three cloves, one-half teaspoon of grated nutmeg, and a small piece of dried chili (if you like it), all together in a salad bowl. Blend small quantities of this mixture by hand, so as to obtain a coarse powder that should be stored in a glass jar.

These herbs marvelously season winter vegetables, omelets, cheeses, and the like.

M.-T. Petit, Pont-de-Cé

DRYING MUSHROOMS

Along with fruits, mushrooms are the best suited for drying. Many mushrooms can be dried on a sheet of paper or wrapping paper. If you pick wild mushrooms, always be certain that you have accurately identified edible ones, because many mushrooms are poisonous.

Cepes (Boletus Mushrooms) on a Screen

VARIATION 1:

Medium or large cepes
Drying apparatus
Cardboard boxes

It's best to use medium-sized or large healthy cepes (boletus mushrooms), because small ones are difficult to cut. Cut the stems and caps separately into thin strips (one-sixteenth to one-eighth inch), and place them on the drying tray. Let dry in the open air, in a warm, very dry place (attic, barn, apartment, or shed), but not in full sun, which is too strong and damages the quality of dried cepes. Drying trays can be stacked. As soon as they are very dry, store the cepes in nonmetallic boxes; tightly closed cardboard boxes are perfect. Store them in a very dry, dark place. Cepes will keep for a few years, but it is best to use them within two years. After that, they tend to turn yellow and to lose their flavor.

To use dried cepes, just soak them in water for a few hours (they regain their original appearance), and prepare them according to your chosen recipe (in a sauce, with a potato dish, or whatever).

Henri Rouy, Cournon-D'Auvergne

VARIATION 2:

Cepes
Wrapping paper or rack

A board covered with wrapping paper and set on a radiator, or a rack hung in a dry, well-ventilated place, can also be used to dry cepes.

Solange and Patrick Cussiez, Aramits
Mireille Lepoetre, Bois-Guillaume

String-Dried Mushrooms

VARIATION 1:

Mushrooms
String
Radiators (steam or wood heat)
Tin cans
Adhesive tape

This method can be used for most mushrooms (except pink mushrooms, which are similar to cultivated button mushrooms), such as morels, cepes (boletus mushrooms), and others.

Sort the mushrooms. Using a knife, remove any grass or soil, but do *not* wash them. Cut them into pieces, and thread them through with a needle and string to make garlands, which you then hang over central heating radiators (we ourselves have wood heating).

Note that electric heating is absolutely inappropriate, as the mushrooms must dry quickly and thoroughly. Let them dry for approximately fifteen days. Unthread them, and store in tin cans, tightly sealed all around with adhesive tape. Label the mushrooms. They will keep this way for at least one year, sheltered from light.

Françoise and Jacques Jeambrun-Ocana, Maiche

VARIATION 2:

Mushrooms
String
Tin cans
Adhesive tape

Garlands of mushrooms can also be dried outdoors or in a dry, well-ventilated room. If necessary, you can finish drying them in a low oven (60°C/140°F). Use tin cans or paper bags to store them.

Miss Rossetti and Mr. Mariani , St. Martin-D'Entrannes
Yves Micheland, St. Marcellin
Florence Besançon, Ramonville
Brigitte Lapouge-Dejean, St. Cybranet

Winter Oyster Mushrooms

Winter oyster mushrooms
Barbecue grill
Woodstove

We cultivate winter oyster mushrooms on wood shavings. Since our yield is seasonal and greater than we can consume, we dry the surplus.

We put the mushrooms on the stainless steel wire shelves in our woodstove. It takes two or three days, over a medium fire, to dry one batch of mushrooms. They must become brittle; then we store them, protected from moisture.

To use them, soak in water overnight, and then cook them as you would fresh mushrooms. With this technique, we can dry oyster mushrooms throughout our growing season, and benefit from a handy source of energy, preserving the taste, aroma, and richness of the mushrooms.

Paul Saillon, Bégard

DRYING OTHER FOODS

Bread

VARIATION 1:

Bread
Wicker trays
Baskets

Right at the last moment when I'm making bread (natural yeast bread made with freshly ground organic whole wheat flour), and after I've kneaded all my dough, I add roasted nuts, hazelnuts, almonds, or sesame seeds.

After baking, I turn the bread out, and let it cool on a wicker tray. The following day, I slice each of the loaves, and place the slices on smaller wicker trays (slices should not touch). I set these trays on top of my kitchen counters. The bread dries in three or four days. Once dry, the bread can be stacked in several layers in a basket, and it will not mold. I store it this way for a month or more. At first, when it is still not too hard, I toast it, and eat it hot. Prepared this way, it is similar to a rusk (biscotti). When it is too hard, I place it on a steamer, or a couscous pot. The steam softens the bread, giving me nice, fresh "cake bread" (as my children call it).

Colette Gilbert, Neuilly-Plaisance

VARIATION 2:

Bread
Paper bread bags
Molds or Pyrex dishes
Tin cans

Cut ½-inch-thick slices of bread, and place them in a large, lightweight paper bread bag (as for French or Italian loaves). Put the bag on a fireplace stone (or failing that, a radiator), and light a fire on two or three consecutive evenings. Better yet, place the slices in molds or Pyrex dishes and leave them out in the summer sun all day. Store the bread in a tin can, and use as needed.

J. and M. Lecoq, Prahecq

Yeast

✤ Successful yeast-making (i.e., natural or "sourdough" starter leaven) does not usually pose a problem, but still, some people prefer to use dried yeast instead.

Yeast
A glass jar

It's not always easy to make yeast from wheat or whole flour, so when we are successful, we don't want any to go to waste. If we make bread regularly, there's no problem; but if that isn't the case, the yeast goes bad, and then we need to start all over again. So this is how I preserve yeast for several months.

I shape the yeast into several small balls, approximately the size of a hazelnut, and put them out to dry in the sun, near a wood fire, or above a radiator. Once the balls have hardened, I grind them to a powder, which I store in a closed glass jar. To use the dry yeast, I add a bit of water to it, then add flour, and within a few days, the yeast "picks up" as though it were fresh.

Lise-Marie Ratier, La Ferrière

Fish Dried in the Ile d'Yeu (Vendée) Manner

Any flat, very fresh fish

Brine

A 24–40-foot pole with cable and hooks at the top

All very fresh flat fish can be dried, as well as somewhat thicker fish, such as mackerel, whiting, pike, or sardine, provided they have been completely cut open and flattened. We dry the fish on a pole (called *vgniou* at Ile d'Yeu) twenty-four to forty feet high, so that flies cannot get to the fish, and where the air and wind dry it effectively. The *vgniou* is a greased pole with a movable ring, so that the fish can be hoisted up using a block-and-tackle system. This ring has hooks all the way around, onto which fish can be secured.

To prepare the fish, cut, scale, wash, and then soak it for twenty-four hours in brine. The salt concentration should be high enough to float a peeled potato. Make lengthwise incisions in the flesh of the fish. Let the fish dry completely over two to three days by hanging it from the top of the pole. The weather should be dry but not necessarily sunny (possible during winter).

To eat the fish, you can grill it over a wood fire, or bake it in the oven, or rehydrate it in a bit of lukewarm water, seasoned or marinated, and cook it just as you would fresh fish. Delicious!

Claude and Marie Bugeon, Ile d'Yeu

Chapter 3

PRESERVING
BY LACTIC
FERMENTATION

Chapter 3

PRESERVING BY LACTIC FERMENTATION

PRESERVING VEGETABLES FOR MONTHS, using neither heat, cold, nor preservatives, yet retaining the original freshness and nutritional value of these vegetables—this is the "miracle" of lactic fermentation.

The process is so easy and effective that we wonder why it has nearly disappeared from use. Still used for making sauerkraut, and for turnips at a few farms in Alsace and in Franche-Comté, lactic fermentation was the primary method for preserving vegetables before heat sterilization was discovered. Let's recall how it is done.

The vegetables are grated or cut up, seasoned with a bit of salt (or a mild brine) and herbs, and left to soak in their own juice. (Salt is the key: A good rule of thumb is about 1½ percent salt by weight of vegetables, which generally translates into two to three tablespoons of salt per quart.)

Lactic microbial organisms—similar to those that curdle milk—develop spontaneously and convert the natural sugars of the vegetable into lactic acid. This environment rapidly acidifies, to the point that it becomes impossible for bacteria responsible for food spoilage to multiply. Vegetables preserved this way will keep in a cool place, such as a cellar, for many months.

This process is remarkable in its simplicity, effectiveness, and beneficial effects on nutritional value and digestibility. For most people who discover them, lacto-fermented vegetables become part of their daily diet and provide year-round access to ready-to-eat raw vegetables. Due to their acidity, however, they should not be eaten in large quantities; they should complement rather than replace cooked and raw vegetables. We prefer to eat lacto-fermented vegetables uncooked, to retain their enzyme and vitamin content, although certain ones, such as sauerkraut, can also be cooked. Once cooked, larger quantities of these foods can be eaten, since cooking reduces their acidity (however, cooking will also destroy some of the nutrients).

One other cautionary note: Don't use tap water in these recipes if it is chlorinated, because chlorine inhibits lactic fermentation. Also, the stones should be noncalcareous, that is, not comprised of limestone, calcium carbonate, or calcium.

For further information about lactic fermentation, see Beatrice Trum Hunter, *Fermented Foods and Beverages* (Keats Publishing, 1973).

✤CAUTION: The USDA and the FDA recommend that all fermented foods should also be canned in a hot water bath to protect against botulism. However, traditional lacto-fermentation methods such as those described here seem to effectively prevent botulism by creating a sufficiently acidic environment. There is good reason to think these recipes are safe without canning. Readers should of course use their best judgment.

SAUERKRAUT

The most popular lacto-fermented vegetable—and the only one known to everyone—is sauerkraut. It is very easy to make at home. The basic recipe does not change, but variations are plentiful. Here are some of the most common:

Sauerkraut in Stoneware Pots

VARIATION I:

2 lbs. of cabbage

1 onion, thinly sliced

5 cloves

1 bay leaf

10 black peppercorns

1 teaspoon cumin seeds

1 teaspoon dill seeds (to taste)

1 heaping teaspoon salt

A stoneware pot or wooden barrel

A clean white cloth

A clean round board (slightly smaller than the pot)

A weight

A large cloth

A rubber band or string

The spices season the sauerkraut nicely, and aid preservation. Note that many recipes recommend about half this quantity of salt.

The most suitable varieties of cabbage are 'Quintal d'Alsace' and 'De Brunswick', (in North America, 'Cheers', 'Tenacity', and 'Atria' are suitable) which have large, firm centers, and therefore are easy to grate.

For a good sauerkraut perfectly preserved, work quickly, and use high-quality cabbage and very clean utensils. Stoneware pots are the most practical, especially those with water seals, specifically designed for lactic fermentation, which eliminate the need for the board, weight, and cloth; however, a wooden barrel that has been thoroughly cleaned may also be used. (Note that the barrel can never be used for any other purpose afterward, as the wood will smell like fermented cabbage.)

Pick cabbage on a nice fall day, after the dew has dried. Remove all the large outer leaves, keeping only the firm centers. If necessary, quickly rinse the cabbage and let it drain on a cloth. Get the pot, spices, salt, onions, and grating utensils ready. (Special graters called "sauerkraut planes" are sold in Alsatian hardware stores, or through the mail, or an electric food processor can be used).

Cut the cabbage in half from top to bottom. Using a sharp knife, make two V-shaped grooves to remove the core. Grate the cabbage centers into thin strips, setting aside two or three nice whole leaves and placing them at the bottom of the pot. Above these leaves, add the first layer of grated cabbage. Using your fists, thoroughly pack down the whole surface. However, take care not to crush the cabbage strips. Depending on the diameter of the pot, add approximately one to two pounds of cabbage at a time, as it is easier to pack in shallower layers. Add the spices, sliced onion, and salt in amounts equivalent to each two pounds or so of cabbage. Continue alternating layers of cabbage with the other ingredients until the pot is full. The cabbage should be soaking in its own juice.

Cover the pot with a clean white cloth. Then place a clean round board, slightly smaller in diameter than the pot, on top of the cloth, and weigh this down (a 2-quart jar of water will do). To protect from insects, cover the board and the weight with a large cloth, secured to the outer rim with a rubber band or string. Keep the pot in the kitchen, or elsewhere at room temperature, for one week, to start the fermentation process. Check the level of the liquid, which must always be one to one and a half inches above the cabbage; this is essential to the preservation process.

Move the pot to the cellar or a cool storeroom. From time to time, check the level of the liquid; if necesssary, add unchlorinated water. The sauerkraut will be ready in six weeks, and will keep until May at least. It can be eaten raw, by itself, or mixed with other raw vegetables, or else cooked. The juice is excellent for your health, and can be used as a replacement for vinegar when seasoning coleslaw. You can also drink this juice, diluted with water.

Each time you take sauerkraut from the pot, you must rinse the cloth, board, and weight, and carefully put them back to keep the sauerkraut well packed and immersed.

It is normal for a white film to form on the surface of the liquid; just remove it gently before taking any sauerkraut.

F. and B. Clergue, Fort-de-France

VARIATION 2:

Approximately 55 lbs. of cabbage

3 large onions

9 oz. salt (or 1 percent of total weight of cabbage)

3 sprigs of thyme

1 handful of juniper berries

1½ handfuls of cumin seeds

3 small sage leaves

3 bay leaves

3 cloves

A stoneware pot

A clean cloth

A few large racks, well washed

Grate the cabbage (or slice into very thin strips with a knife, which is time-consuming and arduous!). Slice the onions into rings. Coat the inside of the pot with salt.

Fill the pot, alternating one 4-inch layer of cut cabbage with one layer of onion rings. Add some salt, a few juniper berries, a few cumin seeds, and the thyme, packing everything down as much as possible. Three times—when the pot is one-quarter, one-half, and three-quarters full—add one bay leaf, one sage leaf, and one clove. Finish with a layer of cabbage, filled to the top. Cover the pot with a clean cloth and a few large rocks. (Well-washed stones from the Rhine work marvelously for me!)

During the first three weeks, the sauerkraut will release water. If the pot overflows, just remove the excess water. During the next three weeks, the cabbage will absorb water, so add more, always preserving the 1 percent salt/

cabbage weight ratio. Ensure that the level of water does not drop below the level of the cabbage in the pot. The sauerkraut will be ready to eat in six weeks.

Turnips, grated with a special grater into long strips, like spaghetti, can be prepared the same way. (In some regions of France, this grater is called *dérouleur de raves,* or turnip streamer.)

Béatrice Sommer, Pfaffenhoffen

Sauerkraut in Glass Jars

Firm cabbage

10 juniper berries, or 1 or 2 bay leaves

1 tablespoon coarse sea salt per jar of cabbage

Hot water

1-quart glass jars with rubber seals

Scald the jars and rubber seals. Grate the cabbage and pack it firmly, adding some of the bay leaves or juniper berries as you fill them.

Top off each jar with one tablespoon of coarse sea salt and a bit of hot, unchlorinated water. With very juicy cabbage, only a few spoonfuls of water are needed.

Close each jar with its rubber seal. Let stand for two to three days in the kitchen, then store in the cellar. Wait one month before eating.

I've been using this method for four years. I'm very happy with it, and I've never lost a jar of sauerkraut yet. My sauerkraut keeps until the following summer, and we even take some with us on vacation. It's very convenient and quite tasty.

I prepare pickles in the same way, sliced if they are large, but stored in smaller jars.

M.-M. Boulo, La Gacilly

Sauerkraut from Whole Cabbage

VARIATION I:

60–70 heads of cabbage

15–17 lbs. coarse sea salt

Horseradish root

2 red beets or 1 red cabbage (optional)

A few carrots or 1 handful of very ripe corn (optional)

A 55-gallon wooden barrel, or a stoneware pot, preferably with a tap

A round wooden board, diameter slightly smaller than the inside diameter of the barrel opening

A clean, heavy, non-calcareous stone

A clean cloth

Buckets

A tube (if barrel has no tap)

This method is used traditionally in the former Yugoslavia. We purposely left it unchanged, even though it may not always be easy to have this much cabbage available, or to find the wooden barrel required for this recipe. In any case, a smaller barrel or a stoneware pot will work fine.

The great advantage to this particular method is that it eliminates the chore of grating. More-over, this type of sauerkraut is far less acidic than that made with cut cabbage.

Choose a good sauerkraut cabbage. The success of your sauerkraut largely depends on the quality of the cabbage. (It's well known that vegetables grown with chemical fertilizers do not preserve as well as those grown organically.) Leave the cabbage untouched for five to seven days after harvesting, so it fully ripens and the leaves soften. (Soft leaves are essential for making *sarmas*, stuffed cabbage leaves traditionally prepared in the former Yugoslavia from lacto-fermented cabbage.)

During this time, prepare the barrel. Brush it carefully and rinse it several times in cold water, then rinse it one last time in very hot water to disinfect it. Let the barrel dry for four to five days in a clean cellar, set off the ground on a wooden support, high enough for any liquid to drain through the tap at its base.

Once the barrel and the cabbage are ready to work with, wash each cabbage and remove the core and any damaged leaves, making sure that no soil or slugs remain. Fill the crevice of each cabbage with salt. Then place the cabbage in layers in the barrel, arranging heads of different sizes to fill any large gaps. Sprinkle each layer with coarse salt; insert several pieces of horse-radish root here and there. For red color, add two peeled red beets, or one red cabbage; for yellow color, add a few carrots or a generous handful of very ripe corn.

When the barrel is full, place the round board, the stone, and the clean cloth (for protection from dust) on top. If your barrel has no tap, insert a tube down to the bottom, leaving the other end accessible at the top, but covered by the board. Leave the cabbage with no added liquid for three to four days, so it will pack down well. Then fill the barrel with cold water, and let the cabbage stand for at least fifteen days before starting to siphon it.

Siphoning serves to distribute the salt evenly, and must be done once a week throughout the fermentation process (four to five weeks). Drain all of the liquid from the barrel to buckets via the tap, and then immediately return it to the barrel. If you're using a tube instead of a tap, suck at the free end of the tube like a siphon to empty the barrel.

During the first few days of fermentation, a light foam may appear on the surface of the barrel. Remove it immediately, and wipe the sides of the barrel with a sponge. You must continue to check for foam during the preservation process, and clean it off as necessary. If you prefer, to make the job easier, insert a cloth between the cabbage and the board to collect the foam; the cloth should be washed each time you open the barrel.

Mrs. Petrovic, Paris

VARIATION 2: SAUERKRAUT FROM ONE WHOLE CABBAGE

1 cabbage

Sea salt

Very hot water

A plate or round board

A stone or other heavy object

A tall glazed container to fit the cabbage

To ferment only one cabbage, this is what you want to do:

Select a tall container of glazed ceramic, and a cabbage that barely fits inside. Clean the cabbage carefully, and remove the core in such a way that the leaves do not come off with it. Sprinkle sea salt in the hole where the core was, and put the cabbage in the container, which you then fill with very hot water.

Press the cabbage down with a plate or a round board, and place a noncalcareous stone or another heavy object, such as a jar filled with water, on top. Leave the container at room temperature (18 to 20°C/64 to 68°F) during the fermentation period, which takes approximately fifteen days.

Mrs. Petrovic, Paris

Sarmas *(Stuffed Cabbage)*

VARIATION 1:

1 medium-sized lacto-
  fermented cabbage

2 medium onions, finely
  chopped

1 heaping teaspoon
  paprika

⅔ lb. ground beef

½ lb. ground pork

1 cup rice, rinsed

A few black peppercorns

Salt, to taste

A large cooking pot with a
  lid

1 or 2 bay leaves

Some bacon or other
  smoked meat (optional)

Sarmas are stuffed cabbage leaves, a traditional Yugoslav dish. A similar dish, *dolmas,* is found in Greece, usually made with grape leaves. For four servings, about twenty *sarmas* are required.

Pick the leaves off the cabbage; if the middle rib is too thick, slice off the excess.

To prepare the stuffing, brown finely chopped onions, then add the paprika and the ground meat. When the meat begins to turn brown, add the rice, and cook slowly for a few minutes. Don't forget to add pepper (a few peppercorns) and salt to taste. Keep in mind that the cabbage leaves are already salted; if they are too salty or too acidic, simply soak them in water until you like the taste. Continue to cook the stuffing, uncovered, stirring constantly with a wooden spoon.

When the stuffing is ready, divide it into portions appropriate to the size of the cabbage leaves. *Sarmas* should be neither too big nor too small (two to two and three-quarter inches long). (When they are too big, they look awkward on a plate, and when they are too small, they suggest that the cook has been penny-pinching!) Place some stuffing on the center of a cabbage leaf, and fold the leaf just as you would a tissue in which you have placed an object.

Line the bottom of a large cooking pot with several cabbage leaves to prevent burning. Put in the *sarmas,* adding pieces of bacon or other smoked meat and bay leaves in between. This will enhance the taste of the cabbage, but it is optional.

Fill the pot with warm water and cook over very low heat. Cooking may take as long as three hours! The longer it cooks, the better it tastes. If you use an earthenware pot, as in the old days, the flavor will be even more exquisite.

Cook partially covered to allow the steam to escape slowly. The *sarmas* will be done when the water has evaporated almost completely.

Mrs. Petrovic, Paris

VARIATION 2: MEATLESS SARMAS

1 medium-sized lacto-
    fermented cabbage

2 medium onions, finely
    chopped

Carrots, finely diced

1 heaping teaspoon
    paprika

2 cups rice, rinsed

1 cup potatoes, diced

Parsley, chopped

Salt, to taste

A few black peppercorns

1 or 2 bay leaves

We prepare meatless *sarmas* in much the same way, but with more rice (about one cup), and with diced potatoes added. For tastier vegetarian *sarmas*, we add finely diced carrots and chopped parsley to the stuffing. First brown the chopped onions, then the diced carrots; then add the paprika, rice, potatoes, salt, and pepper. Cook as described above.

Mrs. Petrovic, Paris

LACTO-FERMENTING OTHER VEGETABLES

Carrot or Beet Juice

Carrots or red beets
Sea salt
A juice extractor
Bottles or canning jars and
  lids

Organic vegetables left in the garden after the winter can be used for this lacto-fermented juice. Juice the vegetables in a juice extractor. Add two teaspoons of sea salt per quart of juice, and mix well.

Pour the juice into airtight bottles or jars. Keep them at moderate room temperature for one week, and then transfer to a cool cellar. After four weeks of fermentation, the juice is ready to drink and is succulent. Success is guaranteed. In my family, people who are ill or convalescing sip this juice before meals.

Anonymous

Cucumbers in Jars

A container for mixing brine

1¼ tablespoons sea salt per quart of water

2 cups bottled spring water or unchlorinated tap water

A few black peppercorns and fennel seeds

1 tablespoon mustard seeds

5–6 cloves garlic

A few onion slices

2 lbs. medium-sized cucumbers, freshly picked and well washed

1 horseradish root, sliced (to keep cucumbers firm)

A few dill (or fennel) flower heads and leaves

1 horseradish leaf (optional)

1½-quart sterilized jar, with rubber seal and fastener

Mix the brine in a separate container; let the salt dissolve in the water while you fill the jar.

Place a few peppercorns, mustard seeds, and fennel seeds in the bottom of the jar, along with the garlic pieces and a few onion slices. Pierce the larger cucumbers with a fork or a toothpick to help the brine penetrate. Put the cucumbers into the jar upright and pack them tightly. As you do so, add the horseradish, mustard seeds, and dill leaves. Place dill flower heads on top of the last layer of cucumbers to keep them from surfacing. Cover everything with a piece of horseradish leaf that you have cut to fit the size of the jar.

Fill the jar with brine, making sure that all ingredients are covered; stop three-eighths to three-quarters of an inch below the rim so the brine doesn't overflow during fermentation. Close the jar tightly; the rubber seal will release any gas produced during fermentation. Starting the next day, bubbles will appear and a sort of foam will form on the surface, signifying that fermentation has begun. Leave the jar in the kitchen for a few days; then store it in a cool place (such as the cellar) when the brine becomes cloudy. Wait approximately six weeks before eating. A perfect way to help digest a heavy meal!

D. Mary, Belgium

Cucumbers in Stoneware Pots

Pickling cucumbers
Grape leaves
A stoneware pot
Dill sprigs
Brine
A board
A clean stone

For this traditional Polish recipe, use large but not quite ripe cucumbers (for example, the 'Northern Pickling' or 'Boston Pickling' variety). They should be about one and a half to two inches in diameter and three to four inches in length.

Wash the cucumbers gently, and put them on clean grape leaves at the bottom of a stoneware pot. In between the layers of cucumbers, put one or two grape leaves and an occasional sprig of dill. Top off with grape leaves. Fill the pot with a boiled and then cooled brine (two tablespoons of salt per quart of water). Cover the pot with a board weighted with a clean, noncalcareous stone to keep insects out.

Pickles can be eaten after about fifteen days of fermentation. They will keep for about two months, if always well covered with brine. A layer of mold may appear on the surface of the brine, but it is harmless.

We eat these delicious pickles just like fresh cucumbers, but they are so full of flavor that they barely need seasoning. They will leave a very pleasant taste in your mouth—a fresh treat for summer's last hot days.

Hélène and Sylvain Jaworski, Fay-de-Bretagne

Sliced Cucumbers

Cucumbers
Salt (1¼ tablespoons for
   2¼ lbs. of cucumbers)
Canning jars and lids

I only peel my cucumbers if their skins are tough. I slice them into thin rounds, and pack them into jars with salt. I fill my jars right up to the rim, as the cucumbers will reduce while fermenting. After a few days, I pack them down, ensuring that none are stuck under the rubber seal. (This would allow air in and would alter the process.)

I preserve large cucumbers in the same manner. No need to peel them. I mix them with raw vegetables (carrots, cucumbers, and so on) to which they add a tasty freshness, particularly in the summer. I use the brine in sauces, as a substitute for vinegar; I also enjoy drinking the brine diluted with some water.

Roger Hombeline, Souvigny

Green Beans

Green beans, freshly
   picked
Salt
Water
Canning jars and lids

Make a brine of two tablespoons of salt per quart of water. Bring to a boil and let cool.

Remove the strings from the freshly picked beans and fill the jars, packing the beans just slightly. (Do not wash the beans unless they are very dirty.) Pour the cooled brine over the beans, right up to the top of the jars. Close the jars with rubber-sealed lids and store them in the cellar.

It is preferable to soak the beans in water overnight to remove the salt before cooking them.

Anne Rogron, Châtillon-sur-Seine

Green Beans without Salt

Green beans
Water
Canning jars

I string the beans, place them uncooked in jars, and cover with cold water. Twenty-four hours later, I discard this water and replace it with fresh water. I repeat this three times, every twenty-four hours. I then move the jars to a cool, dark place.

This unusual process is effective. The beans acquire a tangy taste, similar to that of conventionally lacto-fermented beans.

Roger Hombeline, Souvigny

Lacto-Fermented Green Bean Soup

1 large onion, chopped
4 potatoes, diced
1 bay leaf
1 quart water
Lacto-fermented green beans, cut into 1-inch pieces
2 tablespoons cold-pressed oil
Salt (to taste)

Brown the onion, then add diced potatoes, the bay leaf, and one quart of water. Once this soup base is quite cooked, add the cut green beans, but do not cook them (so you do not destroy their lactic enzymes). To finish, add a little cold-pressed oil, and salt to taste.

Eva Wiehl, Buis-les-Barronies

Lettuce

Lettuce
Salt (2 teaspoons per 2–2¼ lbs. lettuce)
Water
Canning jars and lids

I peel the lettuce, wash the leaves, and cut them into pieces. I place them in jars, alternating each layer with salt, and store the jars in a cool, dark place.

A few days later, when fermentation has begun, I pack the lettuce down. If the volume has reduced, I use one jar to fill up the others, since a full jar will keep better. However, the jars must not be overfilled.

Roger Hombeline, Souvigny

Pearl Onions

Sea salt (1½ tablespoons per quart of water)

Bottled spring water or unchlorinated tap water

2 lbs. white pearl onions

Mustard seeds

Black peppercorns

Bay leaves

2 sprigs of tarragon

Black currant leaves

1-quart sterilized jar with rubber seal and fastener

Mix the brine in a separate container; let the salt dissolve in the water while you fill the jar.

Peel the onions carefully, and scrub them under running water (removing all soil residues). Place a few peppercorns and mustard seeds at the bottom of the jar. Fill the jar with onions, occasionally adding mustard seeds, peppercorns, the bay leaves, and the tarragon.

Fill the jar up to six inches below the rim. Cover the onions with black currant leaves. Add the brine to cover all ingredients. Close the jar tightly. The rubber seal will let out any fermenting gas, as well as any liquid, if the jar is too full!

Leave the jar in the kitchen for a few days until fermentation begins (bubbles appear). When the brine becomes cloudy, move the jar to the cellar to slow down fermentation. The onions can be eaten after six weeks. They taste like onions in vinegar, but are far more delicious.

D. Mary, Belgium

Radishes

Radishes
Salt (2 teaspoons–
1 tablespoon per 2 lbs.
radishes)
Water
Canning jars and lids

I remove any leaves from the radishes, keeping only the roots. I cut winter radishes (pink or black) in half, and cut them again into thick slices. I cut spring (pink) radishes in half, or into several pieces if they are large.

I fill my jars (canning jars with rubber seals) with radishes, occasionally adding a little salt, and packing them down as much as possible. I then store the jars in a cool, dark place.

Three or four days later, I cover the radishes with boiled, salted water (two teaspoons of salt per quart of water), and close the jars tightly.

I use these radishes mixed in with my winter radish salads or with other raw vegetables, or as delicious appetizers. I substitute the fermented brine for vinegar in dressings for raw vegetables, and we drink it diluted with water.

Roger Hombeline, Souvigny

Bottled Swiss Chard Ribs

Swiss chard ribs
Salt (1 teaspoon per 1-
quart bottle)
Water
1-quart glass bottles or
canning jars with corks
or lids

Just as some of us are poets and don't know it, some of us use lactic fermentation and we are not even aware of it! Case in point: this amazing recipe for Swiss chard ribs, lacto-fermented in bottles, with hardly any salt.

This is a traditional recipe from our region (Monts du Forez, at the headwaters of the Loire River). Everyone around here knows about it, yet its use seems to be on the way out (the "frozen-food effect," or perhaps a less independent lifestyle?). This recipe makes dreamers and skeptics of people unacquainted with it.

No one had ever told us that the process was the same as that for sauerkraut (lactic fermentation), but nevertheless, it seemed to us to be so. In any case, the procedure is easy and practical, and the result is delicious.

Why preserve in bottles? Is it because we happened to have some handy, or was there a specific advantage? We don't know. Fruit juice bottles with a wide neck can also be used and are more convenient. Certainly, a glass jar could be used, adding oil on top to make it airtight (as for beans). We've noticed that when oil is used, air bubbles escape, and if the jar is too full, it will overflow during the first month of preservation. We've noticed no such results with bottled Swiss chard.

We have successfully used this method of preservation for seven years, and many of our neighbors use it, too. We never use plastic bottles (wider neck), since we don't trust them (strength, resistance to pressure, hygiene). We once found a glass bottle that had slowly leaked, due to a defective seal, but at first sight, the Swiss chard seemed fine.

We use *bettes vertes à cardes blanches* (an autumn variety of Swiss chard), which hold up better during planting than other varieties. The leaves often end up in our compost pile, because the ribs are far more delicious.

Don't be intimidated by the relatively narrow neck of the bottles. With practice, filling and emptying them becomes much easier. This method is quick and also very flexible (fitting in with both harvest time and your free time), and requires a minimum of preparation (just washing the bottles!).

Sort and cut the Swiss chard ribs into ½- by 1-inch pieces, so that they fit through the neck of a 1-quart glass bottle. Put the ribs in the bottle (which should be placed upright on a mat), carefully tapping the bottle as you fill it to ensure that the chard is well packed. Fill the bottle generously, as chard has a tendency to shrink.

On the first day, top off the bottles with water; on the second day (twenty-four hours later), change the water; and on the third day, before refilling the jar, sprinkle in one level teaspoon of fine salt. (A little more than one teaspoon of salt per bottle doesn't seem to hurt.) During the first three days, Swiss chard loses a little volume and gives off a slightly acrid smell.

Before corking or capping, make sure that as little air as possible remains in the bottle. If necessary, rotate the bottle to chase out any air bubbles. Cork the bottle well (with a solid cork—no holes), or tightly screw on the lid. Then store the bottle on its side in the cellar.

You can eat the chard after one month, and up until the following summer. It's easy to empty the bottle, and takes only a minute if you use a stainless-steel wire bent into a ½-inch hook. Pull out the ribs while holding the neck of the bottle over a colander. When you open the bottle, the chard will have a light, pleasant smell. A 1-quart bottle holds enough to serve three adults. Cook the chard if you like; note that the cooking time will be shorter than for the non-fermented vegetable. Swiss chard ribs are not acidic. Our children dread lacto-fermented green beans, but they love the milder taste of Swiss chard.

Martine Georges and François Barbe, Sail-sous-Couzan

Bottled Swiss Chard Ribs without Salt

Swiss chard ribs
Water
Canning jars and lids

Only the ribs of the chard are preserved. The green leaves are used fresh.

Remove the "strings," cut the ribs into 1¼- to 1½-inch-long pieces, and wash them thoroughly. Place the ribs into widemouthed jars equipped with airtight lids. Pack down and fill the jars with cool water. The next day, rinse the ribs and change the water. Repeat this procedure for four consecutive days, before allowing to ferment.

Preserved in this manner, the ribs will keep easily for one year, and can be cooked like fresh ones.

André Foex, Cleon-D'Andran

Tomato Balls

Ripe tomatoes
Salt
Oil
Herbs
A fine strainer
A finely woven cloth
A screen
Canning jars and lids

For this old recipe from Provence, pick a good amount of tomatoes that have ripened well in the sun. Cut them in half, squeezing lightly to release any water, and put them in a jar. Set the jar outside in the sun (bring them in at night) until they begin to foam and smell a bit fermented.

Pass the tomatoes through a very fine strainer, rubbing it through with your fingers. Collect the strained portion; place it in a clean, finely woven cloth; and hang it outside in the sun until you get a paste dry enough to be shaped into balls. Let the balls dry on a screen in the sun. Then add salt, and put them in a canning jar. Cover them with oil, season with herbs to your taste, and close the jar.

Jennifer Rocchia, Beaurecueil

Tomato Sauce

Ripe tomatoes
Salt
Pepper
Oil
A stoneware pot
A wooden spatula
A fine strainer or loosely
    woven cloth
Bottles

My grandmother passed this traditional recipe down to me, as her ancestors had to her.

Crush the ripe tomatoes with skin and seeds left on in a large stoneware pot. After a day or two (once fermentation has begun), stir them briskly once a day with a wooden spatula, or twice daily, if it looks like the pot will overflow.

As soon as fermentation ceases (it will stop being gassy and bubbly after 5 to 7 days), pass the tomatoes through a fine strainer or a loosely-woven cloth. Keep only the strained liquid, which should be thick and contain most of the pulp. (Straining simply serves to eliminate seeds, skins, and any tough fibers.)

Per one quart of sauce, add one to two tablespoons of salt, and one to two teaspoons of finely ground pepper (to taste). Mix well; put the sauce in bottles, and top with three-quarters of an inch of oil (to the neck of the bottle) for airtightness. Do not cork the bottle, but if you wish, you may cover loosely with a lid.

This sauce will keep perfectly for one year in a dark, cool closet. To use the sauce, remove the oil and any mold, and shake the remaining contents well each time.

This sauce can be used to season pasta, soups, or any other dish.

Jacqueline Magne, Villefranche-du-Périgord

Turnips, Pink Radishes, and Black Radishes

Turnips
Pink radishes
Black radishes
Salt
Spring water
Large clean stones
Jars and lids

I slice or dice turnips and black radishes, leaving the pink radishes whole. I place all this in jars, pack down the vegetables, and place a large stone on top of each jar. I then add brine (two tablespoons of salt per quart of water), made with spring water. Chlorinated water ruins the fermentation process.

I use these "pickles" to accompany vegetable fritters; they add a fresh, acidic taste in contrast to the fritters, which are drier. I also serve them to my guests as an appetizer on wooden sticks.

I reserve the fermented brine for soups or salad dressings; it's an excellent substitute for vinegar.

Colette Gilbert, Neuilly-Plaisance

Zucchini

Zucchini
Salt (2 teaspoons per 2–2¼ lbs. zucchini)
Water
Canning jars and lids

I do not choose particularly young zucchini, but I take them before their skin gets tough, so I won't have to peel them. I grate the zucchini, and put it in jars, alternating each layer with salt. I pack the zucchini down well, fill the jars to just slightly below full with water, and store them in a dark, cool place.

I combine lacto-fermented zucchini with raw vegetables, as it lends a certain freshness to the mixture. It's delicious in a salad made of tomatoes, onions, and fresh zucchini.

Roger Hombeline, Souvigny

VEGETABLE MEDLEYS

Coleslaw in Jars

2 lbs. white cabbage
  (in North America,
  'Cheers', 'Tenacity',
  and 'Atria' are best)

2 large carrots

2 large, firm onions

Black peppercorns

A few juniper berries

Bay leaves

Spring water

Sea salt

1-quart sterilized jar with
  rubber seal and
  fastener

Finely grate the cabbage, carrots, and onions, and combine them well.

Take a very clean jar. Place a few peppercorns, juniper berries, and bay leaves at the bottom. Add two handfuls of the vegetable mixture and pack it down firmly. Sprinkle with salt and more bay leaves, juniper berries, and peppercorns. Stack layers up to one-half to three-quarters of an inch below the rim, packing each layer down firmly. Finish with spices and salt.

Pack down one last time. The vegetables should be covered with liquid. If they aren't, add a brine made with spring water and salt (two tablespoons of salt per quart of water). Tightly close the jar; the seal will allow any fermentation gas to escape, as well as any liquid if the jar is too full. Leave the jar in the kitchen for a few days to launch the fermentation process; then move the jar to a cool place (such as the cellar).

This salad can be eaten after ten days, but it will be quite crunchy. Once the jar has been opened, be sure to pack the ingredients down before reclosing, and do not wait too long before eating because the acid taste will intensify. It is also a good idea to return the jar to the cellar, to help slow down the fermentation process.

D. Mary, Belgium

Mixed Leafy Vegetables

½ lb. onion leaves

½ lb. leek leaves

¼ lb. celery leaves

¼ lb. parsley

⅞ lb. to 1¼ lbs. carrots
(proportion may vary
depending on taste.
The taste of the carrots
will reduce that of the
other ingredients.)

Salt (2 teaspoons per
2–2¼ lbs. vegetables)

Canning jars and lids

I prepare and mix the vegetables, and put them in jars as for my vegetable condiment recipe (see page 89). I use this mixture primarily to season grain pancakes, or to make soups. For soups, I use one to two tablespoons of vegetables per quart of water. I cook them with potatoes, or I cook the vegetables alone and then thicken them with flaked or cracked grains.

Roger Hombeline, Souvigny

Mixed Vegetables in a Glass Jar

3 good-sized carrots

1 celery stalk

2 Swiss chard ribs

12 shallots

2 medium-sized black
radishes, or 2 turnips

Salt

Water

Herbs (thyme, coriander,
fennel)

A glass jar

Wash and scrape the vegetables, and then slice them into ¾-inch rounds or slices.

Make brine (two tablespoons of salt per quart of water). Boil it for five minutes, and let it cool.

Put the vegetables in a jar, add the herbs, and cover with brine to three-quarters of an inch below the rim. Close the jar. Keep it for one week at 20°C / 68°F; then move it to a cool place. You can eat the vegetables after three weeks; they will keep for several months.

Nicole Mansard, St. Julien-Chapteuil

Mixed Vegetables in Stoneware Pots

Assorted vegetables
(onions, beets, carrots,
kohlrabi, red cabbage,
radishes, etc.)

Salt

Water

Stoneware pot with water
seal

Canning jars and lids

In August or September, when the garden over-flows with vegetables, I lacto-ferment them. I dice, slice, or cut the vegetables into strips. I then add a 1 percent (by weight) salt brine, mix everything together, and put it in a stoneware pot with a water seal.

I let the contents ferment for one month and then, since I need the pot to make cabbage or rutabaga sauerkraut, I transfer my fermented vegetables to rubber-sealed jars (I reuse old seals), and store them like that.

They are excellently preserved. Whenever I open a jar, I decant the vegetables to smaller screw-top jars the right size for one meal, so that the vegetables do not oxidize prematurely.

Marie-Claude Jacops, Provenchères-sur-Fave

Vegetable Condiment

Leaves from assorted
  vegetables (parsley,
  carrot, celeriac,
  rutabaga, winter
  radish, turnip, kohlrabi,
  red beet, green onion)

Or root vegetables (carrot,
  winter radish, turnip,
  rutabaga, kohlrabi,
  celeriac, parsnip)

Salt (2 teaspoons per
  2–2¼ lbs. vegetables)

Water

Canning jars and lids

I preserve all kinds of root and leafy vegetables in this way, and then use them to season raw vegetables, grains, and sometimes even cooked vegetables.

When I pull up my winter vegetables, I keep only center leaves (they must be tender), and I remove the middle rib, which is usually stringy. I also discard any roots that are too thin to preserve well without wilting.

I wash and dry the vegetables, then chop them with my old-fashioned all-purpose chopper (you can find them at garage sales). In general, I prefer not to mix the different vegetables, as I prefer to keep each individual taste separate. This way, I can use the condiment best suited to the dish I am preparing. I place the chopped vegetables into jars (sixteen to twenty-four ounces, depending on the quantity to be preserved), pack them firmly, and occasionally add a little salt.

I fill the jars to the usual level (or slightly lower if the vegetables are juicy), so that the liquid won't overflow during fermentation. I finish with a little salt. I then clean the rims of the jars, close them, and store them in a cool, dark place.

Lacto-fermented red beets taste slightly like tamari. Unfortunately, they do not keep for long once the jar has been opened, so I transfer them to small jars. I use the carrots as condiments as well as in pancakes.

Roger Hombeline, Souvigny

LACTO-FERMENTING VEGETABLES A FASTER WAY

This method, widely used in Japan, involves a special glass or plastic container (found in some macrobiotic health-food stores) that has a device for constantly pressing down the vegetables. The vegetables can usually be eaten after a few days of fermentation, and are not intended for long-term storage. Here are just two of the many possible recipes.

Snow Peas and Cucumbers

¼ lb. snow peas
1 cucumber
Ground ginger
1 teaspoon salt
A bit of sake (rice wine)
A bit of soy sauce
Seasoning to taste
Glass or plastic pressure
   jars

Remove the tough parts and string, but do not shell, the pea pods. Cook the peas for two to three minutes in hot water; then dip them immediately in cold water.

Mix the drained peas with sliced cucumber. Put them in a pressure jar and press down.

Eat with a dressing made separately, using the sake, soy sauce, ginger, and other seasonings.

Michel Mangin, Aix-en-Provence

Eggplant and Chrysanthemum Petals

1 lb. eggplant
¼ lb. dried
   chrysanthemum petals
2 or 3 whole cayenne
   peppers
1 tablespoon kombu
   seaweed
2 tablespoons salt
Glass or plastic pressure
   jars

Slice the eggplant into ½-inch thick rounds, and let them dry in the sun for one day.

Finely chop the peppers. Put the chrysanthemum petals at the bottom of the jar, and add salt. Layer, alternating two slices of eggplant with pieces of kombu seaweed, peppers, and salt, until all ingredients have been used.

Press the mixture down firmly in the jar; loosen slightly once the liquid appears. The mixture will be ready to eat in two or three days. Keeping time is limited to about one week.

Michel Mangin, Aix-en-Provence

LACTO-FERMENTING FRUITS

Plums

Plums
Salt
Water
Canning jars and lids

Make a brine with two tablespoons of salt per quart of water. Fill airtight jars with plums (small blue plums, or 'Bonté' or 'Mirabelle' varieties), cover them with brine, seal them, and leave them to ferment. They're delicious!

J. Maitte-Lobbe, L'Hermenault

Plums in Whey

Plums
Whey
Canning jars and lids

Fill a glass canning jar with plums that are not too large (small blue plums, or 'Bonté' or 'Mirabelle' varieties). Cover with cow or goat whey. Close the jar, and leave it as is. The whey will continue to ferment. This will keep for several months.

J. Maitte-Lobbe, L'Hermenault

Sloes

Sloes
Salt
Water
Stoneware pots or glass
    jars

The sloe is the fruit of the blackthorn *(Prunus spinosa)*. Like olives, sloes will keep, left whole, in brine. Pour very salty water over sloes (three tablespoons of salt per quart of water). Preserve them in stoneware pots or glass jars.

J. Maitte-Lobbe, L'Hermenault

❧ Chapter 4 ❧

PRESERVING
IN OIL

Chapter 4

PRESERVING IN OIL

OIL IS A REMARKABLE PRESERVATIVE. Once immersed in oil, many foods will keep almost indefinitely. Preserving in oil, however, has two disadvantages worth noting:

1. The foods become saturated with oil, which cannot be totally removed when eaten, so we risk consuming too much fat if we eat too many foods preserved this way.

2. Oil in general, but especially olive oil (the most suitable for this method of preservation), can be costly.

Nevertheless, preserving in oil has been practiced for a very long time, especially in Mediterranean countries, where olive oil is plentiful and inexpensive. It is particularly well suited to certain foods that are eaten in small quantities, and in any event, are usually cooked with, or in, oil. Mushrooms, certain condiments, tomatoes, artichoke hearts, and eggplant come to mind.

VEGETABLES PRESERVED IN OIL

Artichoke Hearts

20 small artichokes
4 bay leaves
20 black peppercorns
12 coriander seeds
Olive oil
Canning jar and lid

Wash the artichokes well, and cook them in a large pot of salted water for twenty minutes. Remove the leaves and the thistles, keeping only the hearts. Put the hearts in a jar, together with the bay leaves, peppercorns, and coriander seeds. Add olive oil to cover, and close the jar. Marinate for about one month before using the artichoke hearts as appetizers or garnish; they can be kept indefinitely.

Jean-Yves Cousseau, Millau

Eggplant

2 lbs. very small eggplants
Coarse salt
5 cloves garlic
12 pearl onions
1 sprig of thyme
1 bay leaf
Black peppercorn
1 quart oil
A bowl
Canning jars and lids

Slice the eggplant into rounds. Place them in a bowl with a handful of coarse salt, and marinate for six hours in a cool place.

Drain and dry the eggplant with a clean dishtowel. Add the seasonings. Pack the eggplant firmly into jars, cover with oil, and close tightly. Leave the eggplant to marinate at least one month, after which you can serve it as an appetizer.

Myriam Gaignard, Coulans-sur-Gée

Mushrooms

Mushrooms (chanterelles, lactarius [milk caps], etc.)

Wine vinegar

Olive oil

Herbes de Provence (basil, bay leaf, thyme, rosemary, and savory, to taste)

A few cloves of garlic

Tabasco sauce (optional)

A large pot

A salad bowl

Canning jars and lids

Clean the mushrooms and cut them into large pieces.

Boil the vinegar in a large pot. Completely immerse the mushrooms in the boiling vinegar, and bring it to a boil again.

Drain the mushrooms, reserving the vinegar for future uses. When the mushrooms cool, mix them in a salad bowl with olive oil, seasoned to your taste. You can use *herbes de Provence* (an aromatic mixture of basil, bay leaf, thyme, rosemary, and savory), black pepper, red pepper, or whatever; I myself add Tabasco sauce (approximately four tablespoons per twelve jars).

Once you've filled the glass jars with the mushrooms, add more seasoned oil (always ensuring that the mushrooms are well covered), as well as a few cloves of garlic, some basil, and a bay leaf.

As the jar empties, always remember to top off the remaining mushrooms with oil.

This recipe, originally from Calabria (in southern Italy), adds flavor to salads, raw or steamed vegetables, rice, and the like.

Louis Daumais, Manosque

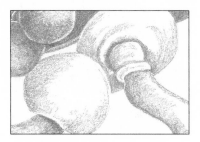

Olives (Green or Black)

Fresh green or black olives
Coarse salt
Olive oil
A nonmetal colander
Canning jars and lids

Pick over the olives, removing the stalks, and pierce each olive with a pin. Place them in a nonmetal colander, adding coarse salt (four tablespoons per two pounds of olives). Then, every day for fifteen days, shake the olives, and add a small amount of salt. This procedure will produce a rather blackish and bitter juice. Following this process, wash and drain the olives, and put them in a jar with olive oil to cover.

Yves Jury and Marie Poscia, Hyères

Cherry Tomatoes

Cherry tomatoes
Small onions or shallots
Cider vinegar or lemon
    juice (1–2 tablespoons
    per 16-oz. jar)
Fresh basil, tarragon,
    oregano, etc. (to taste)
Coarse salt
Olive oil
Canning jars and lids

You must start with cherry tomatoes that are very firm and ripe. If you're using another type, select the smallest ones (no bigger than a tangerine).

Wash and dry the tomatoes. Peel several of the onions or shallots.

Prepare scalded or sterilized 16-ounce jars. Fill them with tomatoes, alternating with a few onions and herbs. When the jars are filled to about one and a half inches from the rim, sprinkle with a pinch of coarse salt. Add one or two tablespoons of cider vinegar or lemon juice, and cover with olive oil.

Close the jars with a very clean lid, and store them in a rather cool place (10 to 15°C/50 to 59°F). The tomatoes will be ready to eat in two to three months and will keep for up to a year. They go well served with grains or with meat.

Anne Duran, St. Front

Vegetable Medley

Very fresh, young vegetables (zucchini, cucumber, eggplant, sweet pepper, carrot, turnip, cauliflower, broccoli, etc.)

Fresh herbs (basil, tarragon, oregano, bay leaves, etc.)

Dill seeds, coriander seeds, and juniper berries (mostly for cauliflower and broccoli)

Vinegar

Salt

Oil

Enamel or stainless steel saucepan

Canning jars and lids

Slice the vegetables in ¼-inch rounds, or dice them. Chop and mix the herbs with the seeds.

Pour enough vinegar into an enamel or stainless steel saucepan to cover the vegetables (you can start off with small quantities). Heat the vinegar until it just starts to boil. Immerse the vegetables in the boiling vinegar for one to three minutes (depending on the texture of the vegetable used). Simmer gently during this time.

Drain quickly and place the vegetables into jars, alternating them with the herb mixture and a pinch of coarse salt. Do not pack the jars too tightly. Pour oil over the vegetables, covering them with a layer about ¼- to ½-inch thick, but allowing an air space of one and a half inches below the rim. Seal with a screw-on lid and store in a rather cool place (10 to 15°C / 50 to 59°F). The vegetables will be ready in one or two months, and will keep for at least a year. Once the jar has been opened, always be sure to top off with a little more oil to ensure that no mold forms.

This recipe is delicious and goes very well with tabouli, couscous, and other grain-based dishes.

Anne Duran, St. Front

Zucchini

Zucchini
Vinegar
Mint leaves
Oil
A saucepan
Canning jars and lids

Choose small, firm zucchini. Wash and cut them in half, or in several pieces if they are large.

Heat enough vinegar in a saucepan to cover the zucchini. Immerse the zucchini in the vinegar as soon as it begins to boil. Immediately remove from the heat, and leave the zucchini to poach for five minutes. Drain and blot with paper towels.

Layer the zucchini in the jars along with two or three chopped mint leaves. Cover the contents of the jar with oil and close it, preferably with a cork. The zucchini will keep for up to one year in a dry, cool place.

Marysette Pastore, Grenoble

CONDIMENTS AND SEASONED OILS

Baguet *(Parsley Condiment)*

1 part shelled nuts
1–2 parts parsley (to taste)
1 part garlic and onion (mixed)
A little vinegar
A few anchovies (optional)
Salt
Olive oil
Canning jars and lids

This is a recipe from Val d'Aoste, in the mountains of northwestern Italy, bordering France and Switzerland. Use it as you would use pesto (basil paste) for seasoning pastas and soups.

Grind all the nonliquid ingredients together very finely. Add the vinegar, put the mixture in jars, and cover it with oil. Without vinegar, preservation is a bit iffy; with vinegar, preservation is a sure thing.

Anonymous

Pistou *(Basil Condiment)*

1 large bunch basil
4 cloves garlic
Salt
1 cup olive oil
Small jars and lids

Pistou is the Provençal version of the more familiar Italian pesto, which usually includes pine nuts.

Grind the garlic and basil, add a pinch of salt, and cover with oil. Mix all the ingredients well and spoon into small jars. You can top off each jar with two or three basil leaves, but make sure that they, too, are covered in oil. The jars will keep very well for more than a year if kept in a cool place.

Bertrand Vallance, Lucenay

Harissa *(Hot-Pepper Purée)*

About 20 hot peppers, preferably fresh red ones

6 cloves garlic

2 pearl onions

1 or more tomatoes (depending on the intensity of the peppers)

Salt

Oil

Canning jars and lids

Mince the peppers, garlic, and onions. Cook half of the mixture along with the tomatoes, reducing until it begins to thicken. Let cool. Add the remaining peppers, garlic, and onions, along with a large pinch of salt. Pour the mixture into jars, and add oil to cover. Store in a cool place.

This spicy sauce traditionally accompanies couscous, meat, fish, soups, and other North African dishes.

Sophie Jacmart, Coux

Herbs in Oil

Herbs (parsley, nasturtium leaves, basil)

Salt

Cold-pressed sunflower or olive oil

Canning jars and lids

I make this recipe using sunflower oil to preserve parsley and nasturtium leaves, and using olive oil to preserve basil; but it could certainly be used for other herbs, such as chervil.

I chop the herbs as finely as possible, and add two teaspoons of salt per two pounds of herbs. I then put this mixture in a jar with a tight-fitting lid. As I fill the jars, I try to avoid allowing in too much air, but I don't pack the herbs too tightly, so that the oil can penetrate them.

Next, I pour in three-quarters of a cup of cold-pressed oil for every one-quarter pound of herbs. The oil must saturate the mixture, but a thin layer should also remain on the surface. If it doesn't, I pack the mixture down a little to allow the oil to rise to the surface. I close the jars, and store them in a cool, dark place.

I use these herbs in salad dressings, to season vegetables and grains, and to spread (in very small quantities) on bread.

Once opened, the jar can keep for a while, if it is stored in a cool place and if a film of oil always remains on the surface.

Christine Roger, Switzerland

Tomato Purée

Tomatoes
Salt
Olive oil
Aromatic herbs
Canning jars and lids

Cook the tomatoes in very little water. Drain and pass them through a strainer. Heat the resulting purée, adding the salt. Reduce it until very thick (about thirty minutes), stirring constantly over low to medium heat.

Let the purée cool. Shape it into balls about the size of a walnut, and put them in a jar filled with good-quality olive oil and aromatic herbs. The balls must be totally submerged.

Marie-Françoise Lavigne, St. Ismier

Seasoned Oil

Herbs (thyme, rosemary, basil, savory, tarragon, etc.)
Garlic
Shallots
Olive oil
Bottles with caps or corks

Put herbs, garlic, and shallots into a bottle, and add the olive oil to nine-tenths full. (This is done to prevent overflowing when the oil expands with heat.) Leave the bottle in the sun for about three to four weeks, and then use it as is. It is a delicious flavoring with which to season your winter dishes!

Annie Dijoud, St. Joseph-de-Rivière

CHEESES IN OIL

Goat Cheese

VARIATION 1:

10 small, dry cheeses
  (Saint-Marcellin or
  petits chèvres)
1 sprig of rosemary
2 sprigs of thyme
1 bay leaf
10 black peppercorns
2 small hot red peppers
Olive oil
Canning jars and lids

Place cheese into a very clean jar. Add the herbs, peppercorns, and red peppers. Cover with oil and close.

Eric and Sylvie Courtille, Lacapelle-Marival

VARIATION 2:

Goat cheeses or broccio
2 cloves garlic

You can also prepare fresh goat's cheese (add two cloves of garlic) or broccio (cheese made with ewe's whey) in the same manner.

Florence Besançon, Ramonville
J. Y. Cousseau, Millau

VARIATION 3:

Small goat cheeses
Herbs (thyme, oregano,
  wild thyme, savory)
Olive oil
48-oz. canning jar and lid

Use small, not too ripe goat cheeses. Roll each one in a mixture of herbs: thyme, oregano, wild thyme, and savory, for example.

Put the cheeses in a large glass jar (about forty-eight ounces), and cover them with olive oil. Wait at least four months before eating the cheese. This seasoned oil can also be used to flavor salads, particularly tomato salads.

Anonymous

Drained Cottage Cheese

Cottage cheese, preferably unsalted
Oil
Canning jar and lid

Preferably use an unsalted cottage cheese, which takes longer to ferment. Pack the cheese tightly into a jar with a rubber seal, leaving as little air as possible. Fill to one to one and a half inches from rim.

Pat down the surface of cheese, and pour three-eighths of an inch of oil over it. Wet the seal and close the jar. Store in a cellar. The cheese will keep for three or four months.

Jean Roger, Jully

Chapter 5

PRESERVING IN VINEGAR

Chapter 5

PRESERVING
IN VINEGAR

THE PRINCIPLE USED IN THIS TYPE OF preservation is similar to that of lactic fermentation: The environment created is too acidic to support the growth of microorganisms. The difference here is that acid (acetic acid from vinegar) is added to the food to encourage preservation, rather than occurring as a by-product of the fermentation process.

Compared with lactic fermentation, preserving with vinegar has two distinct disadvantages:

1. We miss out on certain benefits that derive from fermentation: the synthesis of enzymes and vitamins, easier digestion, and medicinal properties.

2. Foods taste very acidic and can only be eaten in small quantities.

On the other hand, preserving in vinegar offers distinct practical advantages:

It is a quick, easy, and safe method. So it is not surprising that vinegar has been used for a very long time as a preservative, particularly for aromatic herbs. Its most common applications today—for gherkins, pearl onions, and other pickled vegetables—are for the most part, just variations of lactic fermentation, whose use predates that of vinegar for preserving food. In particular, pickles were always lacto-fermented in times past, and then transferred to vinegar solely to stabilize them for commercial purposes.

Yet, preserving in vinegar remains an interesting and worthwhile method in its own right, especially for herbs, fruits and vegetables eaten as condiments, and certain kinds of fish. Vinegar also is a preservative agent in sweet-and-sour preparations, which are covered in chapter 8.

❧Be sure to use unchlorinated water in these recipes, as chlorine will ruin the process. Once you have opened a container of food preserved in vinegar, store it in the refrigerator.

VEGETABLES IN VINEGAR

Beets

2 lbs. small beets
1 quart white wine vinegar
6 black peppercorns
½ teaspoon cracked pepper
1 small red bird pepper
20 fresh white pearl onions
Two saucepans
Canning jars and lids

Cook the beets in boiling salted water for twenty to twenty-five minutes or until tender. In another saucepan, combine the vinegar with all of the pepper. Bring this mixture to a boil and cook it for two minutes. Remove it from the heat, and let the pan cool.

Peel the pearl onions. When the beets are done, let them cool only slightly, peeling them while still warm. Put them in a jar with the onions, and pour in the seasoned vinegar.

Let the contents cool before closing the jars. Store them in a cool place. The beets will be ready to eat in about two weeks.

Myriam Gaignard, Coulans-sur-Gée

Brussels Sprouts

Brussels sprouts
Water (unchlorinated)
Wine vinegar
Olive oil
A saucepan
Canning jars and lids

Clean the brussels sprouts and soak them for five minutes in boiling water. Pack them in jars with a mixture of equal parts water and wine vinegar. Top off with a layer of olive oil and close the jars. Rinse the brussels sprouts before you eat them.

Sylvie and Bruno Jouin-Dubost, Melesse

Cabbage Compote

1 head of cabbage
Salt
1 quart wine vinegar
2 quarts red wine
A cloth
A stoneware pot
A plate or round wooden board that fits the interior diameter of the pot
A large rock

This recipe is a variation of the lacto-fermented compote traditionally prepared in Drôme.

Wash and pull off the leaves of the cabbage and allow them to wilt on a cloth for twenty-four to thirty-six hours.

Layer the cabbage leaves in a stoneware pot; salt them moderately at every sixth layer. Place a plate weighted with a large rock over the top layer of cabbage in order to pack down the leaves. Cover the cabbage with vinegar and wine, and let it marinate for one month.

Rinse the cabbage carefully before using it. Drain and cut the leaves into strips. Serve them with a vinaigrette dressing, by themselves, or with potatoes.

Martine Brown, Châteauneuf-Du-Rhône

Cherry Tomatoes

2 lbs. cherry tomatoes or small, very firm red tomatoes

6 tarragon leaves

4 cloves

6 white peppercorns

6 coriander seeds

2 pinches of sea salt

1 quart vinegar

Thin needle

A large canning jar or two small ones and lids

Wash the tomatoes, without removing the stems, if possible. Dry them carefully with a cloth, and pierce them in two or three spots with a thin needle.

Wash and blot dry the tarragon leaves. Put the tomatoes in a large jar (or two small ones), along with the tarragon, cloves, peppercorns, and coriander seeds. Add the salt and pour in the vinegar. Seal the jars airtight and store them in a cool, dry, and dark place.

Wait approximately six weeks before eating. These tomatoes are excellent accompaniments to cold or hot poached fish, as well as a variety of terrines and grains dishes.

Patrick Eude, Le Havre

Gherkins in Cider Vinegar

Gherkins, 3–4 inches long

Seasonings (to taste: tarragon, mustard seeds, pearl onions or shallots, bay leaves, cloves)

Cider vinegar

Coarse salt

A large bowl

A cloth

A saucepan

Canning jars and lids

Sprinkle coarse salt over freshly picked cucumbers and let them stand overnight in a large bowl to release excess water. The next day, dry them well with a cloth (not necessarily one by one!). Put them in a jar, packing them tightly. In a saucepan bring the cider vinegar to a boil. Add the seasonings and pour boiling cider vinegar into the jar. Fill it to the rim, and immediately seal it airtight.

Gaby Ingrand, Les-Sables-D'Olonne

Glasswort

Glasswort
Cider vinegar
A colander
A saucepan
Canning jars and lids

Pick the glasswort, quickly rinse the stems, and drain them in a colander. Do not add salt, as glasswort is naturally very salty (it grows in salt marshes). Put the stems in jars and cover them with boiling cider vinegar. Seal airtight, immediately.

Cider vinegar allows glasswort to retain its special flavor. The vinegar can be used for vinaigrette dressings, for rabbit in mustard sauce, and in place of plain vinegar in other recipes. I reuse my screw-top jam or honey jars, and in this way keep my pickles and glassworts from one year to the next.

Gaby Ingrand, Les-Sables-D'Olonne

Green Peppers

Green peppers
Wine vinegar
Salt
A bowl
A cloth
Glass or stoneware jars

Coarsely chop fresh peppers, sprinkle them liberally with salt, and soak them overnight in a bowl. The next day, spread the peppers on a cloth to drain.

Fill either glass or stoneware jars with the peppers, and cover them with wine vinegar. They will be ready to eat after about one week, and will keep for several months. They can be served with cold cuts, stews, and so on.

Irène Clua, Durban-Corbières

Horseradish in Vinegar (or Olive Oil)

Horseradish root
Vinegar (or olive oil)
Canning jars and lids

Peel the horseradish root and grate it very finely. (The tears will flow!) Fill glass jars and cover the horseradish with good vinegar (or olive oil). Close the jars. Horseradish served in either vinegar or oil (depending on what you are serving) will keep indefinitely.

Jacqueline Closset, Belgium

Nasturtium-Seed "Capers"

Nasturtium seeds
Dill leaves (optional)
White wine vinegar
Small jars and lids

I grow a lot of nasturtiums in my garden. From their seeds, I prepare these "capers" which everyone likes!

Toward the end of summer, collect the green seeds from nasturtiums that have lost their blossoms. Put these into jars along with the dill leaves and a good white wine vinegar. The taste and shape are somewhat reminiscent of capers. These are delicious with ham, bread, and butter.

Florence Coantic, Dieulefit

Pearl Onions

2 lbs. fresh white pearl
onions
Salt
1 quart vinegar
12 black peppercorns
10 cloves
1 bouquet garni (see p. 24)
6 coriander seeds
A large bowl
A colander
A cloth
A saucepan
A cheesecloth or strainer
Canning jars and corks

Immerse the onions in boiling water, drain, and peel them. Then place them in a large bowl, sprinkle them with salt, and marinate for twenty-four hours. Shake the bowl from time to time, so all the onions become saturated with the salt.

The next day, rinse the onions quickly under running water, drain them, wipe them with a cloth, and put them into jars. Boil the vinegar and herbs in a saucepan for five minutes; remove from heat and let cool.

Filter the vinegar through a cheesecloth or strainer, and pour it over the onions. Seal the jars, preferably with a cork. The onions will be ready to eat in approximately fifteen days, and will keep for at least one year.

Maryselle Pastore, Grenoble

Radishes

Pink radishes
Cider vinegar
A few onion slices
One or two lemon slices
A few black peppercorns
A saucepan
Canning jars and lids

Clean and dry the radishes, leaving just a bit of the stalk intact. In a saucepan, boil the cider vinegar for approximately one to two minutes to concentrate it. Let it cool, uncovered.

Put the radishes in a canning jar, mixing in a few onion slices, one or two lemon slices, and a few black peppercorns. Pour in the cooled vinegar. Close airtight.

Allow the radishes to stand three months before using them.

The red pigment of the radishes blends with the vinegar, giving it a nice pinkish color. These radishes make an unusual but delicious condiment for cold meats, especially grilled or smoked ones, or for salads and rice (slice them first), for example.

Anonymous

Tomatillos

Tomatillos
Vinegar

These are round, green fruits similar to small tomatoes, and are produced by a plant whose papery husks resemble the flowers of the ornamental plant, Chinese lantern [*Physalis alkekengi*, known in France as *lanternes-de-Venus* ("Venus's lantern") or *amour-en-cage* love in a cage.] Tomatillos can be used as you would use tomatoes (see recipe on p. 112). When they are small, tomatillos preserve very well in vinegar.

J. Maitte-Lobbe, L'Hermenault

White Button Mushrooms

White button mushrooms
Vinegar
Red pepper
Bay leaf
A few coriander seeds
A saucepan
Canning jars and lids

White button mushrooms are as perfect for pickling as gherkins are.

Wash the mushrooms, removing the soil-end of the stems. In a saucepan, bring the vinegar to a boil. Put the mushrooms into sterilized jars, adding the herbs and spices. Fill the jars to the rim and pack well. Pour in the boiling vinegar, let the jars cool, and close them tightly.

Myriam Gaignard, Coulans-sur-Gée

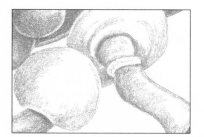

SEASONINGS IN VINEGAR

Basil

Basil
Cider vinegar
Small jars and lids

To keep basil fresh for salads, all you have to do is chop some and place it in a small jar with some good cider vinegar. Store the jar in a cool place, and enjoy this valuable seasoning anytime!

Jacqueline Clossett, Belgium

Pickled Garlic

1 lb. garlic
1 quart water
1 tablespoon salt
Bay leaves
Black peppercorns
1 cup vinegar
½ cup water
¼ cup sugar
A saucepan
Small jars and lids

Peel the garlic. Boil one quart of water with one tablespoon of salt. Add the garlic and continue to boil for three to five minutes. Drain the garlic.

Fill small jars with the garlic, one bay leaf, and five black peppercorns.

Boil the vinegar along with one-half cup of water and sugar, pour this mixture over the garlic, and immediately close the jars. The garlic will keep for a very long time, and is particularly tasty in salads.

Ted Braam, Hagraulet-Du-Gers

Sage or Rosemary-Scented Vinegar

1 lb. dried sage or
   rosemary flowers
½ quart wine vinegar
A glass jar or bottle with
   cork or lid
A fine cloth
Bottles with corks or lids

Soak the dried flowers in a glass jar filled with wine vinegar. Close the jar and leave it in the sun for eight to ten days. Then filter the contents through a fine cloth, twice. Store this fragrant vinegar in tightly closed bottles.

Michel Guerville, Dannes

FRUITS IN VINEGAR

Cherries

Sour cherries (such as
  'Montmorency'
  variety)
Cider vinegar
A cloth
A saucepan
Canning jars and lids

Wash the cherries and cut the stalks to one inch long. Drain the cherries well by spreading them on a cloth. Put them in a jar, and cover with cider vinegar that you have previously boiled and cooled.

Wait at least one month before using these cherries.

Elisabeth Schubel, Besançon

Bicolored Grapes

1 lb. white grapes, in
  bunches
1 lb. black grapes, in
  bunches
2 sprigs of tarragon
6 white peppercorns
4 cloves
1 tablespoon sugar
1 quart wine vinegar
A cloth
Canning jars and lids

Wash the grapes while still in bunches; then choose the biggest grapes, and remove them with scissors, leaving a short stem attached. Dry each grape carefully with a cloth. Wash and blot dry the sprigs of tarragon.

Layer the grapes into jars, alternating both colors, and adding the peppercorns, cloves, and tarragon. Add the sugar and cover the grapes with vinegar. Close the jars airtight, and store them in a cool, dry, and dark place for about six weeks before using.

Both sweet and sour in taste, these grapes go impeccably well with poultry or game terrines.

Patrick Eude, Le Havre

Cinnamon Dark Red Plums

2 lbs. dark red plums
1 quart cider vinegar
⅓ cup brown sugar
6 cloves
1 cinnamon stick
1 tablespoon pink
    peppercorns
A cloth
A needle
A saucepan
Canning jars and lids

Choose plums that are not too ripe. Wash and dry them carefully with a cloth. Pierce them with a needle in three or four places, right down to the pit. Put the plums in jars.

Pour the vinegar into a saucepan. Add the brown sugar, cloves, and cinnamon; bring this to a boil for five minutes. Remove the pan from the heat and add the pink peppercorns. Carefully pour the hot vinegar over the plums, until they are well covered. Let the jars cool, close them tightly, and store them in a cool, dry, and dark place.

The plums will be ready to use in about four weeks. Sweeter than most condiments, they are exquisite with cold meats, stews, and other hearty dishes. Without the cloves and pink peppercorns, they can even be used as a pie filling.

Patrick Eude, Le Havre

OTHER FOODS IN VINEGAR

Anchovies in Aged Wine Vinegar

Fresh anchovies
Salt
Aged wine vinegar
Garlic
Parsley
Olive oil
Deep plate or bowl

Split the anchovies and remove the spines. Spread them in a deep plate, sprinkle with salt, cover with vinegar, and marinate for twenty-four hours.

Rinse the anchovies very quickly, drain them, and dry them carefully with a cloth. Arrange a layer of anchovies in a salad bowl or a deep plate, and generously sprinkle them with chopped garlic and parsley. Continue layering anchovies, garlic, and parsley until you've used up all these ingredients. Cover everything with the olive oil.

It's best to eat the anchovies within ten to fifteen days; they are delicious with tomatoes or potatoes

Irène Clua, Durban-Corbières

Hard-Boiled Eggs in Wine Vinegar

Hard-boiled eggs
Wine vinegar diluted with ⅓ water
Tarragon (optional)
A few black peppercorns
Canning jars and lids

Shell the hard-boiled eggs and put them into a jar, along with the tarragon and peppercorns. Cover with diluted wine vinegar, and close the jar. These eggs can be eaten after two or three days, but do not keep longer than about fifteen days. Delicious with raw vegetables.

Pascale Dey-Marquis, Montigny-en-Gohelle

❧ Chapter 6 ❧
PRESERVING
WITH SALT

Chapter 6

PRESERVING
WITH SALT

ABOVE A CERTAIN CONCENTRATION of salt in food, microorganisms cannot develop and thus the preservation of food is assured.

While preserving with salt seems a relatively ancient process, it is not as old as the methods we have described so far. At one time, salt was mainly used for preserving meat, fish, and butter; every rural household had a salt tub. Today, salt still is used for fish, such as cod or anchovies, as well as for pork and butter. Among vegetables, we sometimes salt green beans, herbs, and vegetable mixtures for soup stock.

There are two main disadvantages to preserving food with salt:

1. The salt must be removed from most foods before consuming them,

which usually requires lengthy soaking and repeated rinsing that also eliminate some of the nutrients;

2. If the salt is not completely removed, we risk consuming more than is considered healthy these days.

However, for preserving foods that we eat in small quantities, or that don't need much soaking and rinsing, salt has its place. It is one of the best ways to preserve fish, for which other methods tend to be less convenient. Green beans seem to be the vegetable that best lends itself to being preserved with salt. There are many versions of this method of preservation, and we have included in this chapter several of the most common ones. Yet, among all the foods preserved with salt, mixed vegetables are perhaps the most appealing: no salt need be removed; they do not cause you to eat too much salt; and they make instant stock for soup.

VEGETABLES IN SALT

Grape Leaves (for stuffing)

Grape leaves
Coarse salt (2 parts salt to 1 part water)
Water
A saucepan
A glass jar
Camembert box

Make a brine of the salt and water; bring to a boil. Scald the grape leaves, ten at a time. Roll them up and then pack them tightly in a glass jar. Pour in the brine and cover the jar, using the inverted bottom of a Camembert box (or another thin wooden box) that has been well covered with brine. Use the leaves as you need them; rinse with water to remove the excess salt. The Greeks and Turks stuff grape leaves with ground lamb and / or rice mixed with a little olive oil, lemon, and herbs, for *dolmas*.

Anne-Marie Arrouye, Aix-en-Provence

Bottled Green Beans

Green beans
Salt
Oil
Widemouthed jars

String and wash the beans. Pack them tightly in jars (preferably with a wide mouth) and cover with water. Change the water every day for three days.

On the fourth day, replace the water with a brine made of one-half cup of salt to one quart of water. Finish with a capful of oil and close the bottles.

Mr. Buisson, Riorges

Green Beans in Brine

Green beans
Salt
A saucepan
A stoneware pot

Make a brine using one-half cup of salt to one quart of water. Boil and let it cool. String, wash, and blanch the beans in boiling water for five minutes, and let them cool. Put them in a stoneware pot, cover them with brine, and check now and then to see that they are always well covered in brine.

Soak the beans in water for a few minutes just before cooking them.

Marie-Françoise Lavigne, St. Ismier

Green Bean Halves with Coarse Salt

Green beans

Coarse salt (1 cup per 2 lbs. of beans)

A bowl

Canning jars and lids

Break the beans in half, and put them in a bowl with the salt. Leave them to marinate for three days, stirring occasionally.

Next, put the beans into canning jars (used rubber seals are okay). Fill the jars to the top and seal them. Do not transfer any liquid from the bottom of the bowl to the jars, nor should you remove any salt from the beans as you pack them in.

These beans will keep for three years. To use them, rinse the beans under the tap, before parboiling in a large quantity of water. Rinse the beans once again under the tap, and then finish cooking them.

Maurice Valle, Neufchâtel-en-Bray

Green Beans in a Salt Pot

Green beans

Table salt

An earthenware or stoneware pot or wooden barrel

Use only young and tender green beans, preserving them as you harvest them. Using the following method, they taste as good as fresh ones, and much better than frozen ones. Another great advantage: You don't have to prepare all the beans in one day.

Put some salt in the bottom of a clean container (an earthenware or stoneware pot, or a wooden barrel). Fine table salt is best, but coarse salt will do.

Quickly wash and dry the beans. Remove the stems and the strings. Put a layer of beans in the container, packing them down carefully but firmly with a wooden stick or a bottle.

As you harvest additional beans from your garden, continue adding salt and beans in alternating layers until the container is full. Cover the container and store it in a cool place. Eventually, a brine will form, soaking the beans. Do not discard this brine—it's the essential ingredient in the preservation process—but from time to time remove any film that has appeared on the surface.

When winter comes, use the beans as you need them. Rinse first in cold water for five minutes; then soak for two hours (not longer). Cook as usual.

Martine Saez-Mercadier, Camarès

Tomato Purée

Tomatoes
Salt
Oil
A food mill
A cheesecloth
A large bowl
8-oz. jars and lids

Wash the tomatoes carefully, removing the stems. We then put them through a small food mill (from Italy), which separates the skin and seeds from the pulp and juice. A Foley food mill will work.

Next, we filter the pulp and juice through a cheesecloth. When only a well-drained thick purée remains, we place it in a large bowl, and add the salt (approximately one tablespoon per quart of tomatoes). We put this paste into small jars, add a small amount of oil, and close the jars. We keep them at the bottom of our refrigerator.

We've been using this method for three years and find it very successful. We tried lactic fermentation, but found that the flavor changed and not everyone liked it. Using this method, the taste remains the same.

Incidentally, 'Roma' tomatoes keep well, whole, in salted water (two to two and a half tablespoons of salt per quart of water).

Louis Lagrave, Carmaux

Whole Tomatoes

Tomatoes
Olive oil
Salt
A saucepan
Glass jars and lids

Make a brine (one-quarter cup salt to one quart of water), and bring it to a boil. Allow to cool. Choose firm tomatoes, preferably ('Campbell' variety, for example), wash and dry them carefully, and put them in glass jars. Pour in the cooled brine, up to one and a quarter inches below the rim, and fill in the remaining space with olive oil to cover. Close the jars airtight and store them in a cool place.

These tomatoes will keep for nine to ten months; use them for sauces.

Jean-Yves Cousseau, Millau

Migaine de Thézou *(Mixed Vegetable Stock)*

1 lb. leeks
1 lb. tomatoes
1 lb. onions
¾ lb. parsley and chervil, mixed
½ lb. turnips
½ lb. celery
1 lb. salt
A meat grinder (or food processor)
A bowl
Jars

This recipe came from a grandmother in my village.

Grind all ingredients coarsely together in a meat grinder (or a food processor). Let the mixture stand overnight in a bowl in a cool place. The next day, remix the contents of the bowl by hand. Put the ground vegetables in jars, and store them in the cellar or some other cool place.

While this mixture will keep for up to three years, it is best to use it all within the first year, since you can replenish your stock with fresh ingredients the following September. I add one or two tablespoons each time I make soup, tomato sauce, court-bouillon [stock for poaching fish], and so on. I prefer to toss it in raw, for a more interesting texture, but it can be cooked, too.

Anne-Marie Franc, Baccarat

Verdurette *(Vegetable Stock)*

½ lb. parsley
½ lb. chervil
½ lb. celery
½ lb. leeks
½ lb. sea salt
Jar

Chop the herbs, mix them with the salt, put the mixture in a jar, and close it airtight. Store in a cool, dark place. This mixture is excellent for seasoning soups during the winter. You can also add all kinds of vegetables (carrots, celeriac, and Swiss chard, for example). Adjust the preceding proportions accordingly.

Yields two pounds of *verdurette.*

Mrs. Jouaville, Laxou

OTHER FOODS IN SALT

Anchovies

Fresh anchovies
Salt
Jar

Gut, clean, and wash the anchovies. Fill a jar by alternating layers of anchovies and salt. Make sure to sprinkle enough salt to completely cover each layer of anchovies. Seal the jar. After several days, the jar will be full of brine; you can use the anchovies in about two to three months' time. They will keep for one year at room temperature.

Mireille Carentz, Bouzonville

Preserved Lemons

10 organic lemons

½ cup salt

Hot red peppers, fenugreek seeds, and cardamom pods (optional)

An earthenware pot or airtight glass jar

Wash and then soak the lemons in cold water for two to three days, changing the water several times. Drain the lemons; then partially quarter them lengthwise, leaving the ends intact. Slide one teaspoon of salt into each lemon, and store them all in an earthenware pot or airtight glass jar. Cover the lemons with water that has been boiled, then cooled. Seal the pot or jar and wait one month before consuming.

Lemons preserved this way will keep for a very long time. You can also add hot red peppers, fenugreek seeds, cardamom pods, or other spices to your taste.

Preserved lemons, an essential ingredient in Moroccan and other Mediterranean cuisines, provide a refined zest in meats and couscous, as well as in salads. Take one or two from the jar; rinse; and use them whole, sliced, or chopped fine. Some people prefer to discard the tangier pulp, using only the rind.

Sophie Jacmart, Coux

Rose Petals

Rose petals

Salt

Canning jar and lid

Pick the rose petals before 10 o'clock in the morning, selecting flowers that are both scented and very open. Fill a jar, alternating layers of petals and layers of salt. Close airtight.

The moisture in the petals will be absorbed by the salt, and consequently, the petals will not rot. You need only to open the jar to fill the room with a subtle rose scent.

Jean-Pierre Paulin, Sassenage

Chapter 7

PRESERVING
WITH SUGAR

❧ Chapter 7 ❧

PRESERVING
WITH SUGAR

S UGAR IS A PRACTICAL AND ECONOM-
ical method of food preservation—so
much so that we tend to overindulge,
and make jams that contain more sugar
than fruit! When we discover that excess
sugar is one of the great scourges of the
modern diet, we might think it best to
renounce jams completely. Besides, replac-
ing white sugar with brown sugar is only a
relative improvement. Whole or raw sugar
(evaporated juice from sugar cane) would
be a better substitute, but its strong flavor
often masks the taste of the fruit.

The solution to this problem is twofold:
avoid eating too much jam and other sugary
foods, and make these foods using far less
added sugar, or none at all. Knowing and
applying these techniques, we can continue
to preserve food properly and successfully.
For example, certain jams made with very

little sugar must be refrigerated once opened, preferably in small jars, to prevent premature spoilage.

For those recipes that require sugar, we will use either brown or whole sugar. Other recipes are "sugar-free," or use honey instead.

Note that the term "sugar-free jam" in essence is a contradiction in terms, since by definition, sugar is the preservative agent in jams. To be more precise, we should discuss "jams with no *added* sugar." In reality, jam already contains sugar: both glucose and fructose, which naturally occur in all fruit.

Jams with no added sugar were not invented by health-food advocates wanting to reduce their sugar consumption. These preserves are an old tradition dating back to a time when sugar was scarce and expensive (or even nonexistent). Three classic examples, and the most commonly known jams of this type, are *pommé* (apple jelly), *poiré* (pear jelly), and *raisiné* (grape jelly). The first two have been made for centuries in certain regions of northern Europe, particularly Belgium and Germany, whereas the *raisiné* is a tradition of Périgord in southwestern France. Carob "honey" is a similar preserve that is found in the Middle East, Galilee (recipe follows in this chapter). All these preserves share this common feature: They are made from the juice only, and not from the whole fruit. Thus, they are jellies or thick syrups, rather than jams. Their preparation is based on this simple principle: Prolonged cooking evaporates enough water to concentrate enough of the naturally occurring sugars for preservation to take place. Jams from whole fruit can also be prepared by following the same principle.

In general, after pouring hot jam or jelly into a jar and sealing it, turn the jar upside down. This will sterilize any air remaining in the jar and ensure preservation. It's also a good idea to store the jars upside down.

JAMS

Apple Jam with Raisins

10 lbs. apples

¾–1 lb. (to taste) raisins, not too small

3¾ lbs. sugar

1 vanilla bean

1 cup water

A preserving pan or a large saucepan

A piece of muslin

Canning jars and lids

Peel and core the apples, wrapping the peelings and seeds in a piece of muslin tied into a knot. Quarter the apples and put them in a preserving pan, together with the muslin sachet, sugar, and vanilla. Add the water and cook the mixture over low heat, allowing the sugar to dissolve slowly and without sticking.

Continue cooking; add the raisins after one hour. Put the jam in jars while it still is hot. Screw the lids on and turn the jars upside down to ensure proper preservation.

Excellent served over semolina cake.

Brigitte Lapouge-Dejean, Domme

Blackberry Jam

2 lbs. blackberries

⅔ lb. diced apples, rather tart (pippin type)

1½ lbs. sugar

⅓–½ cup lemon juice

½ cup ground hazelnuts

A large saucepan

Canning jars and lids

Combine the blackberries, apples, sugar, and lemon juice, and let this sit overnight in a cool place.

Prepare the jars before cooking. Use screw-top jars and scald them carefully, along with their lids. Drain on a cloth.

Bring the blackberry mixture to a boil and continue cooking it over rather high heat for fifteen minutes. Add the hazelnuts after the first ten minutes.

Fill the jars to the rim with the hot jam, screw the lids on tightly, and immediately turn the jars upside down. If the jars are properly full, very little air should remain at the top. Store the jars upside down in a cool, dark place.

This process sterilizes the jam, which keeps perfectly well with this low sugar content.

Mrs. Drezet-Théroud, Rouffignac

Black Currant Jam with Honey

Black currants
Honey (same weight as
  the fruit)
An enamel saucepan
A wooden spoon
Canning jars
Beeswax or paraffin

Pick the currants when they are about ready to fall. Place them in an enamel saucepan, rinse them, and pick them over. Do not add water. Cook the currants over high heat for thirty-five minutes, stirring constantly with a wooden spoon; then turn the heat off.

Leave the cooked currants standing as is, including the peels, seeds, any and berries that are still whole. Add the honey to the saucepan (liquid honey or not, in the same quantity as the fruit). The honey should not cook; it simply needs to be stirred and well mixed in.

Put the jam in jars. When they are cooled, top them off with ³⁄₁₆ inch of beeswax or paraffin.

Martine Siegfried, Brantome

Elderberry Jam

Elderberries, very ripe
Sugar (1⅓ lbs. per 2 lbs.
  of fruit)
A large saucepan
A food mill
Canning jars and lids

Rinse, seed, and then cook the berries for a few minutes. Pass through a food mill to eliminate any remaining seeds.

Weigh the puréed elderberries, and add the sugar accordingly. Cook this mixture for one to three hours, depending on the intensity of the heat. You can reduce the quantity of sugar if you increase the cooking time. Pour the jam into jars and seal.

This jam will remain quite liquid. For a thicker jam, you may choose not to pass it through a food mill, and retain the seeds, which are similar to hazelnuts in taste.

Sophie Jacmart, Coux

Melon Marmalade with Mint

Melon

Sugar (1 lb. per 2 lbs. of pulp)

Fresh mint (10 leaves per 2 lbs. of fruit) finely shredded

A large saucepan

Canning jars

Choose very ripe melons. Cut them open, scoop out the seeds and any fibers, and remove the rind. Chop up the remaining fruit.

Cook the melon with sugar in a large saucepan. After thirty minutes, add the finely shredded mint leaves, and continue cooking until you obtain the desired consistency. When a drop of marmalade congeals on a cold plate, it's ready to put into jars.

Colette Jobez, Pierre-de-Bresse

Pear Jam with Cinnamon

2 lbs. pears

1⅓ cups brown sugar

1 cinnamon stick

A preserving pan or large saucepan

Canning jars and lids

Peel, core, and cut the pears. Add the sugar and cinnamon. Cook until the mixture has liquefied and falls in small drops from a spoon. Put in jars immediately; close and turn the jars upside down several times, to sterilize any air inside. This way, you get a jam with little sugar content that will keep all winter.

E. and T. Courtille, Lacapelle-Marival

Pear Jam with Walnuts

10 lbs. pears

Sugar (use half the weight of the peeled and cored pears)

4–5 lemons

50 fresh walnuts

A large saucepan

A piece of muslin

A colander

A skimmer

A preserving pan or large saucepan

A wooden spoon

Canning jars

Plastic wrap and rubber bands

Pour four quarts of water and the juice of two lemons into a large saucepan. Peel the pears and let them stand in this water so they won't brown. Then quarter the pears, saving the cores and seeds in a knotted piece of muslin.

Drain the pears well and weigh them to determine the amount of sugar required (half as much of the weight of fruit). Crack the walnuts and chop them coarsely.

Fill a large saucepan halfway and add the juice of half a lemon per quart of water. Bring this to a boil and immerse half the pears. Poach them for three minutes in simmering (not boiling) water; then remove the pears carefully with a skimmer, making sure not to break them. Repeat the operation with the remaining pears.

Now prepare the syrup: Put the sugar into a preserving pan; add water (two cups for every two pounds of sugar). Bring it to a boil over medium heat until the sugar melts; then increase the heat and boil for another five minutes. Next, immerse all the fruit, and the muslin containing the cores and seeds, in this syrup. Simmer for fifty minutes, stirring gently two or three times with a wooden spoon. Add the walnuts and cook for five more minutes.

Pour the still-hot jam into scalded and then dried jars, filling them almost to the rim. Wipe the outside of the jars, and cover the tops with squares of plastic wrap. Secure with a rubber band.

Pierrette Donati, La Ciotat

Baked Mirabelle Plum Jam

8 lbs. mirabelle plums (or any other variety of plum)
1 lb. sugar
A large baking dish

Pit the plums, add the sugar, and bake uncovered in a low oven (150°C/300°F), stirring from time to time. The jam will reduce by about half. It's absolutely delicious!

Marie-Claude Jacops, Provenchères-sur-Fave

Greengage Plum Jam with Walnuts

4 lbs. greengage plums
2 oranges, finely chopped
Juice of 2 grapefruits
3 lbs. sugar
1 cup raisins (pitted)
½ cup walnut halves
A preserving pan (or large saucepan)
Canning jars and lids

Wash and pit the greengages. Cut each plum in quarters and soak these overnight along with the sugar, raisins, and grapefruit juice.

The next day, cook the finely chopped oranges—including the rinds, pulp, and all of the juice—in one-half cup of water for thirty minutes.

Put the soaked pears into the preserving pan over low heat. When this boils, add the cooked oranges and the walnuts. Cook for twenty minutes more. When the jam is done put it into jars.

Anne-Marie Bouhelier, Clermont-Ferrand

Mirabelle Plum Jam with Apples

10 lbs. mirabelle plums (or any other variety of plum)
4 lbs. sugar
2 lbs. summer apples
A preserving pan or large saucepan
A piece of muslin
Canning jars and lids

Pit and then soak the plums in a preserving pan along with the sugar. Let them stand in a cool place for several hours.

Peel, core, and quarter the apples, saving the peelings and seeds, and wrapping these in a piece of muslin tied with a knot. Put the apple quarters and the muslin sachet in the pan with the plums.

Cook, stirring regularly and gently, as the fruit will tend to stick toward the end of the cooking process. Pour into jars, seal, and store.

Brigitte Lapouge-Dejean, Domme

Porvidl *(Dark Red Plum Jam)*

4 lbs. dark red plums
1¾ cups sugar
¾–1 cup cider vinegar
A porcelain or
  earthenware container
Canning jars
Plastic wrap

Mix the plums with the sugar and vinegar in a porcelain or earthenware container. Stir well, cover, and let stand for twenty-four hours in a cool place.

Cook the mixture over low heat for one and a half hours, stirring from time to time.

When cooled, close the jars with plastic wrap, and store them in a cool, dry place.

Providl will keep very well; use it to garnish crêpes and various cakes (such as linzertorte).

Alice Halbwax, Creutzwald

Marinated Rosehip Jam

VARIATION 1:

Rosehips (fruit of the wild rose)
White or red wine (optional), or water
Sugar
A preserving pan or large saucepan
A food mill
Canning jars and lids

This jam is seldom made, unfortunately. It's true that you have to gather rosehips during the winter, after several frosts have softened them. The cold and the wild-rose thorns take their toll on your fingers, and the preparation for this jam takes quite a bit longer than for most other kinds.

Having said this, the delicious taste and velvety smoothness of rosehip jam make it all the more worthwhile! Rosehips are also very rich in vitamin C (one-half pound of rosehips contains as much as is found in two pounds of lemons).

The Causses region, where I live (in extreme south-central France) is poor, but covered with wild-rose bushes. Every year, I partake of frozen, silent mornings, for the pure pleasure of giving my friends this glowing nectar to savor.

Pick the rosehips when they are very soft (January or February, depending on the winter). Remove the black tip from each end, place the fruit into a preserving pan, and cover it with a good white or red wine. Marinate one week, stirring every day. (You can leave out the wine and omit this marination step, cooking the rosehips with just enough water to cover them, but the flavor of the jam will be different. Jams made with white wine or red wine also taste different from each other, but they're both a treat!)

After one week, cook the contents of the pan over high heat for fifteen minutes. Then put the rosehips through a food mill, using a fine grind (this is the longest part of the process, due to the quantity of seeds in rosehips).

Weigh the purée obtained and add one and two-thirds pounds of sugar per two pounds of purée. Cook this mixture for thirty minutes, stirring constantly. Put the jam in jars and seal them. The consistency of the jam will vary from year to year; some years it comes out firmer than others.

Emmanuelle Bompois, St. Énimie

VARIATION 2:

Rosehips
Sugar
A large saucepan
A food mill
Canning jars and lids

Gather the rosehips when they are very ripe, immediately after the first frosts. Sort and wash the rosehips, if necessary. Immerse them in boiling water for a few minutes; then put them through a food mill with the cooking water, using a fine grind. Weigh the puréed rosehips, and add one and one-third pounds of sugar per two pounds of purée. Cook this until thick enough. Put it in jars, closing them immediately.

The normal consistency of this jam is thick, but it will become very hard if you cook it for too long.

Sophie Jacmart, Coux

Uncooked Rosehip Jam with Honey

Rosehips
Liquid honey
A food mill
Canning jars and lids

Pick the rosehips after the frost, when they've become soft. Wash them, remove the stems and the black tips, and purée the fruit in a food mill. Using the back of a knife, scrape off the purée that comes out. This process may seem long and tedious, but it's worth it.

Mix the purée along with an equal amount of liquid honey.

This jam is very rich in vitamin C and will keep indefinitely. You can serve it as a garnish on desserts, cakes, and so on.

Odille Angeard, Cognin

JELLIES

Uncooked Jellies

Fruit (all types)
Sugar (1 lb. per 2 lbs. of pulp)
A fine strainer
10-oz. canning jars and lids

I make this jelly with strawberries, raspberries, blueberries, and even pitted ripe cherries, apricots, greengage plums, or peaches. Pass the fruit through a fine strainer, extracting only the pulp. Slowly stir in the sugar. The jelly is ready when it "folds over" while stirring (like a thick cream). Pour it into medium-sized jars (ten ounces) and store in a cool place. You can use this jelly to flavor milk, yogurt, ice cream, and so on. It's excellent!

Donald Grégoire, Grans

Uncooked Red Currant Jelly

Red currants
Honey (3¼ cups per 2 lbs. fruit)
A terrine
A wooden spoon
Canning jars and lids

Crush the fruit to obtain the juice, and let it stand. When a deposit has formed on the bottom of the terrine, decant the clear top layer, and filter it. Add the honey, stirring with a wooden spoon for fifteen minutes. When the mixture becomes more fluid, pour it into glass jars. Close and store them in a cool place. This jelly will keep for two to three months.

Michel Mangin, Aix-en-Provence

Cooked Jellies

Fruit (all types)

Sugar (1 to 1¾ cups per quart of juice)

Agar-agar (½ teaspoon per quart of juice)

A juice extractor

A preserving pan

A wooden spatula

Canning jars and lids

Wash the fruit and pass it through a juice extractor to obtain as much juice and pulp as possible. Remove the peels and seeds, and pass the remaining mixture through the extractor once again, to obtain the maximum amount of liquid.

Weigh the liquid to determine the amount of sugar to use (25 to 40 percent of the weight of the juice, depending on the fruit and your taste) and pour the liquid into a preserving pan. Bring it to a boil and add the sugar. Stir with a wooden spatula for five minutes, allowing the sugar to completely dissolve. Add the agar-agar (diluted in a bit of water), and boil for five more minutes while stirring. Remove the pan from the heat and, using a ladle, pour the hot liquid (watch your hands!) into previously scalded jelly jars. Screw the lids on (also scalded), and turn the jars upside down immediately.

Let cool. When the jelly is set (after fifteen to twenty-four hours), place the jars right-side up again. This will create a vacuum, which is necessary for good preservation. Store the jars in a cool, dry place.

These jellies will keep for one year. Due to the short cooking time and the method used to extract the juice, they are very tasty and not too sweet.

Sylvie and Bruno Jouin-Dubost, Melesse

Sea Buckthorn Berry Jelly

Sea buckthorn berries

Sugar or honey (1 lb. per quart of juice)

1–2 tablespoons of flour

A large saucepan

The thorns of the most common bush on northern France's dunes hide a berry that is a gold mine of good health—if one risks being pricked. Pick the berries before the first frost. They are rich in vitamins C (more so than lemons), B, and E; carotene; and calcium.

Because the berries crush easily between the fingers, it is best to pick them using scissors. Eating them raw or drinking their juice is most beneficial; however, they can also be made into a jelly by crushing them to yield a juice.

Reduce one quart of juice with one pound of sugar or honey, until it reaches a syrupy texture. If necessary, add one or two tablespoons of flour for thickening.

Michel Guerville, Dannes

NO-ADDED-SUGAR AND OTHER PRESERVATIVES

Apple-Pear Molasses

1½ lbs. apples and/or pears

Juice extractor

Canning jars and lids

This recipe comes from Germany, where we often find it on the tables of people who like sweets without the added sugar. You can spread this molasses on a slice of toast, or use it to flavor and sweeten pies, for example.

You can use damaged fruit, but keep only the good parts. With a juice extractor remove the juice, and bring it to a boil over low heat. Simmer for several hours, stirring regularly, until the water evaporates. The resulting syrup may become very thick. Pour it into jars while hot. It will keep well without sterilizing.

Yields one half cup of molasses.

Josette Claisse, Rouvenac

Carob "Honey"

Carob beans (fresh, dried,
  or powdered)
Water
1 tablespoon olive oil
A grinder or flat rocks
Buckets or containers
Jute bags
A fine strainer or screen
A large stewpot

This "honey" takes a long time to prepare and is used mainly by people living in Mediterranean countries. However, by purchasing dried or powdered carob beans from a store, you can skip the first step, which makes the preparation much easier.

Harvest the carob beans and dry them in the sun on a flat surface for approximately one month. Wash the beans in water, and dry them once again in the sun (simple drying, this time). Pick them over, getting rid of any beans that are wormy or empty (these feel much lighter in your hand than the others). Grind the beans, using a grinder or by rubbing them between two rocks. The drier the beans are, the easier it is to grind them, and the more water they will absorb during the next stage of this recipe. We bring our carob beans to a flour mill in town that also grinds carob, but many villagers here in Galilee use rocks to grind them.

For the next stage, fill buckets or other containers up to three-quarters full with the ground carob beans. Cover with water (about four inches over the beans). Soak for twenty-four hours, stirring three or four times, and adding water if necessary; the beans must remain covered with water at all times. Put this mixture into jute bags, and hang the bags from beams with a container placed beneath each bag. The juice that drips from the bags will collect in the containers. Allow the bags to drain for twenty-four hours.

The carob "honey" is made only from the juice that drips from the bags. Pass this juice through a fine strainer or screen, pour it into a large stewpot, add one tablespoon of olive oil, and bring the liquid to a boil. Boil gently to allow the excess water to evaporate. Stop cooking the mixture when it reaches the desired texture, which varies widely according to individual tastes.

We cook the juice of the carob beans on a wood fire in the backyard. For about twenty quarts of juice, we allow five hours of cooking time to obtain "honey" that is fairly liquid. We've also noticed from experience that the olive oil prevents the liquid from overflowing during the lengthy boiling period, and keeps the carob "honey" from picking up the smell of smoke when cooking over a fire.

The residue left in the bags can be used as animal feed (poultry, sheep, and so on) or as fertilizer. We use it to fertilize our olive trees.

Here in Galilee, carob "honey" is still in great demand and very much appreciated. Many villagers use it to sweeten hot beverages or pastries. It is also easy to spread and is delicious served on toast.

The Photini Sisters, Galilee, Israel

Liège *(Apple and/or Pear) Syrup*

Apples and/or pears
A juice extractor
A large copper pan
A stoneware pot or glass
    jars
Paper or lids

Use ripe fruit. Cook it in a little water and pass it through a press to extract the juice. Pour the juice into a large copper pan and cook it, stirring regularly, until it becomes thick. Test for doneness by letting a drop of syrup fall into a cup of cold water; if the drop stays intact, the syrup is ready.

Pour the syrup into a stoneware pot (or glass jars), let cool, and cover with good paper (or lids). The syrup will keep for several years.

Cooking time will depend on the amount of juice. For example, for fifty quarts of juice, you will need at least ten hours of cooking over low heat. For smaller quantities, the cooking time is shorter.

Jacqueline Closset, Belgium

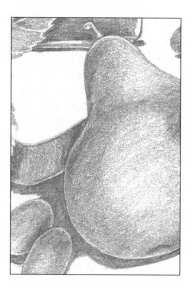

Pear Jam with No Added Sugar

Pears
A stewing pot
A wooden spoon
Canning jars and lids

One year I had to go away, and when I returned, I found quite a few pears on the ground, all somewhat bruised. I peeled them, keeping only the good parts, which I then cut into small pieces (about ⅜ inch on a side). I put the pears in a stewing pot only partially covered, and cooked them over low heat, without adding water or sugar. I stirred them from time to time. After a few hours, they were soaking in their own juice. I then removed the cover and turned up the heat, continuing to stir from time to time, so the liquid would evaporate and the pears would cook slowly. After several hours of cooking, the texture began to thicken, at which point I let them cook over high heat for five more minutes. I then immediately poured the pears into scalded jars and sealed them. This pear purée was delicious spread on toast. It also kept for several years.

G. Petrelli, Pontaillier-sur-Saône

Pommé (Apple-Quince Jelly with No Added Sugar)

2 parts apples
1 part quinces
1 teaspoon cinnamon per
  2 lbs. of fruit
A saucepan
A piece of cheesecloth
A strainer
Canning jars and lids

Cut up the fruit and cook it in a bit of water. Tie up the seeds in a piece of cheesecloth, and add them to the fruit to cook for three hours. The next day, add the cinnamon, and cook the fruit for an additional two and a half hours. Remove the cheesecloth, strain the fruit, and cook it for another two and a half hours. Put the jelly into jars.

Anonymous

Whole Fruit Jam

VARIATION 1:

Very ripe fruit (any type)

A preserving pan or large saucepan

Canning jars and lids

This method is good for all types of fruit, including grapes, greengage plums, and so on. Use fruit that is very ripe; simply cut and crush it roughly. Bring the fruit to a boil; then cook it over very low heat for a very long time.

It is impossible to recommend a precise cooking time, since this depends on the type of fruit used, and its ripeness and water content, both of which vary from one year to the next. In any case, you should allow as much water as possible to evaporate. Stir often, because certain fruits have a tendency to stick during cooking. The jam is ready when it does not run off of the spoons but forms a bead that sticks to the spoon. At this stage pour the jam into scalded screw-top jars. It will keep for at least two years.

VARIATION 2:

Red currants or other acidic fruit

Honey or raisins (½ weight of fruit)

For red currants, for example, you can add honey; for other very acidic fruit, you can add raisins (about half the weight of the fruit); or you can mix fruits.

J. Maitte-Lobbe, L'Hermenault

SYRUPS, FRUIT PASTES, AND OTHER CONFECTIONS

These preparations are very sweet, even though the quantities of sugar are less than those conventionally called for. Consume them in moderation.

Black Currant Syrup

8–9 lbs. black currants

2 qts. wine

Sugar (3¾ cups per quart of juice)

A food mill

A piece of cheesecloth

A large saucepan

Bottles and corks, or canning jars and lids

Wash and peel eight to nine pounds of black currants. Pass them through a food mill using a spinach grater (medium setting). Soak the currants for forty-eight hours in two quarts of wine. Extract the juice by pressing the mixture through a loosely woven cloth; then add the sugar.

Cook the juice and sugar in a large saucepan over low heat. When the sugar melts and the syrup starts to boil, skim it off, and pour it into bottles. Cork the bottles the following day, and store them in a cool place.

Yves Micheland, St. Marcellin

Candied Angelica

Angelica

A large pinch of salt

Sugar (same weight as the angelica)

Water (half as much as sugar)

Vegetable brush

A preserving pan or large saucepan

Porcelain, earthenware, or glass jar and lid

Pick young and pulpy angelica stems that do not need much peeling. Remove the largest, cut them into pieces four inches long, and then scrub them with a brush. Put them into a preserving pan with cold water, and cook over high heat until the stems are tender. Remove from heat. Add a large pinch of salt, to make the angelica turn green again. When cooled, drain and weigh the angelica.

Prepare the syrup (two parts of sugar for one part of water), and boil together for a few minutes. Pour the hot syrup over the angelica.

The next day, drain the angelica. Reserve the syrup, and boil it to reduce it. Pour it, still boiling, over the angelica. Repeat this procedure every day for three to five days, until the syrup has reached the "soft ball" stage, or a temperature of 120°C/250°F.

There are two ways to store the candied angelica:

1. You can leave it in the syrup in a closed porcelain, earthenware, or glass jar.

2. You can drain it, wipe off the excess sugar, and let it dry on a screen for a few days, protected from insects. It will keep indefinitely in a storage container.

Pascale Dey-Marquis, Montigny-en-Gohelle

Candied Chervil

Chervil

Sugar (same weight as the chervil)

Salt (½ teaspoon per 1 lb. chervil)

Water (1 cup per 1 lb. sugar)

A preserving pan or large saucepan

Drying screens

Canning jars or cans

Gather large, very tender stems before they have grown leaves. Cut lengthwise into pieces measuring two and one-quarter to three inches. Weigh these, and immediately place them in cold water. They should be completely covered.

Boil the chervil until the pulp begins to bend under your finger. Remove the pan from the heat and add one-half teaspoon of salt per pound of chervil. Let this solution sit for one hour; the chervil will regain its nice green color. Drain.

Make the syrup using one cup of water per pound of sugar. Boil this syrup, stirring constantly, until it reaches 29° (Brix scale) on the syrup thermometer (a hydrometer that determines the amount of sugar in a solution). Pour the syrup over the chervil, and let stand for twenty-four hours.

Remove the chervil from the syrup. Boil the syrup once again until it reaches 32° and pour it over the chervil. Let stand for another twenty-four hours.

Remove the chervil again. Boil the syrup a third time, until it reaches 33°. Pour it while still boiling hot, over the chervil. This time, let it stand for forty-eight hours.

Drain the chervil, and let it dry on screens in a warm place. Then store it in jars or cans, also in a dry place. Candied chervil provides a delicious and unusual taste (somewhat like aniseed) in cakes, and can also be used to garnish roast pork.

E. Lepoetre, Bois-Guillaume

Fruit Paste

Fruit (quinces, pippin
    apples, apricots, black
    currants, etc.)
Sugar (2 lbs. per 2 lbs. fruit
    purée)
A saucepan
A food mill
Flat molds
Cellophane wrap

Chop the fruit and cook it in very little water.
Put it through a food mill, using a very fine
grind. Drain the purée as much as possible. Add
the sugar (amount equal to the weight of the
purée). Reduce this mixture by cooking it over
low heat for thirty minutes, stirring constantly.
(Wear long oven mitts to avoid burns on your
arms.)

Spread the paste in flat molds (such as lids
from tin cookie boxes). When the paste is dry,
you can cut it into sticks or squares. After it sets,
I cover the paste with a cellophane wrap made
specifically for jams.

For Christmas, I cut black currant paste into
small squares, which I then dip into chocolate. A
treat for young and old a like!

Marie-Françoise Lavigne, St. Ismier

Fruit in Syrup

Fruit (any type except
    greengage plums)
Water
½ cup of sugar per 2 cups
    of water (or less)
A large saucepan
6¼–7-inch-diameter
    stainless steel saucepan
Wooden spoon
Canning jars and lids

Prepare the fruit: Peel, remove stems, quarter,
and pit, if necessary. Have the following ready
to go on your stove: a large saucepan half-filled
with water, in which to scald the jars and lids;
and a stainless steel saucepan in which you've
mixed the water and sugar to heat for the syrup.
Use one-half cup of sugar or less per two cups
of water.

Heat the water-sugar mixture. When the
syrup begins to boil, add just enough fruit to fill
the jars, which meanwhile are soaking in hot
water in the other saucepan. The syrup will stop
boiling temporarily. Bring the fruit in the syrup

to a boil, and stir gently with a wooden spoon. Do *not* let the fruit boil longer than one minute.

Take the hot jars out of the water, drain them, and fill them to the rim with fruit and syrup. Take the hot lids, and drain those. Close the jars and turn them upside down immediately. Let stand this way until cooled, but store right-side up.

TIPS:

✢ Once in the syrup, the fruit must not boil for more than one minute.

✢ Do not use greengage plums; they burst as soon as you immerse them in the syrup.

✢ Use commercial glass jars (jam or honey) along with their reusable lids.

✢ You can also use jars with glass tops and rubber seals; don't forget to scald the rubber seals first.

Marcelle Ninet, Gex

Raspberry Syrup

2 lbs. raspberries
1 quart red wine
1½ lbs. sugar per quart of juice
A strainer
A thick-bottomed saucepan
Bottles and corks, or canning jars and lids

Soak the raspberries in red wine, well covered, for two days in a cool place. Press them through a strainer, and add the sugar. (The original recipe required two pounds of sugar per quart of juice; however, by using only one and a half pounds, the syrup tastes even better and will keep just as well.)

In a thick-bottomed saucepan, bring the mixture to a boil; them simmer for two minutes. Fill the bottles and close them immediately, so as to sterilize the air remaining inside. Analyses have indicated that less than one-half of 1 percent of alcohol remains per quart.

Laurence Bretin, Corcieux

Rhubarb Syrup

Rhubarb
Sugar (½ lb. per pound of
   juice)
A large saucepan
A piece of cheesecloth
Bottles and corks, or
   canning jars and lids

Wash the rhubarb stalks without peeling them; cut into small pieces, and cover with water. Cook the stalks over medium heat for about thirty minutes.

Strain everything through a piece of cheesecloth, and weigh the juice collected. Use half as much sugar, by weight, as juice. Cook the sugar in a little water. When it reaches a boil, add the strained rhubarb juice, and cook the mixture over low heat for fifteen minutes.

Pour the syrup into bottles and close tightly. Wait at least two weeks before using (with water, as for any other syrup), so it is more flavorful. The pulp remaining in the cheesecloth can also be cooked with some sugar to make jam.

Mrs. Risler, Boulogne

Chapter 8

SWEET-AND-SOUR PRESERVES

Chapter 8

SWEET-AND-SOUR PRESERVES

T HE COMBINATION OF SWEET AND sour flavors within the same dish derives largely from Asian—particularly Indian, Chinese, and Indochinese—cuisine. We mainly encounter this blend of flavors in condiments, such as Indian chutneys *(chatni)* or English ketchup (which originally came from China but—like chutney—grew popular in Europe during the colonial era).

Long ago, these condiments were not intended to be preserved; in fact, most of the time, chutneys were prepared right at mealtime in India. These days though, sweet-and-sour condiments are almost always preserved, which accounts for the sizable quantities of vinegar and sugar used in their preparation (unless they are pasteurized or sterilized). However, these condiments nearly always are variations of the original recipes.

All chutneys share a similar foundation: In traditional recipes, they seldom contain sugar; their sweet taste comes from the fruit itself. As for the sour taste, this often comes from lemon juice, and not vinegar. But chutney without sugar or vinegar will not keep, so today's recipes require both, and often in rather large quantities. In this chapter we present only sweet-and-sour recipes that use as little sugar and vinegar as possible.

Chutneys can be very spicy and usually accompany cold meat (as do pickles). They also go very well with boiled potatoes, rice or other plain grains, and various salads. We also have recipes for ketchup, pickles, fruit, and other preserves.

Jeannette Busiaux, L'Étang-la-Ville

CHUTNEYS

Chutneys with Little or No Added Sugar

2 lbs. fruit and/or vegetables

⅓ cup brown sugar

1 cup vinegar

Salt, spices, herbs (to taste)

Baking soda

A clean cloth

2 large saucepans

Canning jars and lids

Wash and chop the fruit and/or vegetables. Put them in a large saucepan, along with the spices, and boil over low heat. When this mixture is soft and well blended, add the sugar and vinegar, and continue to boil until you obtain the desired consistency (like that of jam, or more liquid, if you prefer). Total cooking time is about three hours.

During this time, prepare the jars; you can use screw-top ones. Wash them in boiling water with baking soda, rinse thoroughly, and drain (upside down) on a clean cloth. Boil the lids for five minutes, once again using baking soda; rinse carefully, and let stand in clean water.

When the chutney is ready pour it into the jars, and close them immediately. The taste improves with age. We eat chutneys cold with all kinds of dishes. In India, you always find chutneys on a *thali,* an individual round tray on which the meal is served. Here are recommended fruit, vegetable and seasoning combinations for some of our favorite chutneys:

APPLE CHUTNEY

2 lbs. apples

1 lb. onions

Salt, ginger, mustard seed, cayenne pepper, cloves

GREEN TOMATO CHUTNEY

2 lbs. green tomatoes

¾ lb. sour apples

1 lb. onions

½ lb. celery

Salt, ayenne pepper, oregano

MEDITERRANEAN CHUTNEY

(our favorite!)

2 lbs. ripe tomatoes

1 lb. onions

3 cloves garlic

1 zucchini

1 eggplant

Salt, black pepper, red pepper, coriander, tarragon, rosemary, marjoram

PLUM CHUTNEY

2 lbs. plums

1 lb. apples

½ lb. onions

¼ cup black radishes

1 clove garlic

½ lb. tomatoes, very ripe

Salt, ginger, cayenne pepper

POTIMARRON CHUTNEY

2 lbs. *potimarron* (Japanese winter squash, see p. 20)

1 lb. apples

1 lb. onions

¼ cup black radishes

Salt, ginger (1 tablespoon), cayenne pepper, bay leaf, black pepper, cloves, cinnamon

RHUBARB CHUTNEY

2 lbs. rhubarb

¾ lb. onions

Salt, ginger, curry

Renée Verhoeff, Simorre

Green Apple and Green Tomato Chutney

4 lbs. green apples

2 lbs. green tomatoes

10–15 white pearl onions

1 tablespoon English dry mustard

½ lb. sugar

2 cups wine vinegar

3 teaspoons salt

3 teaspoons ground pepper

1 small hot red pepper, chopped

A Dutch oven

A large saucepan

Canning jars and lids

Chop the apples and the tomatoes. Mix them with the salt and let sit for twenty-four hours. Drain and then cook the apple-tomato mixture in a Dutch oven over low heat for twenty minutes. In saucepan, boil the onions, the mustard, and the other ingredients for a few minutes. Then add the apple and tomato mixture, and cook for forty-five minutes.

Put this mixture in screw-top jars. This chutney will keep for many years, and makes an excellent accompaniment for many dishes, including grains.

Jacqueline Closset, Belgium

Onion Chutney

1⅔ lbs. onions

1 tablespoon butter

2 tablespoons ginger root (or ground ginger)

1 banana

4 level teaspoons curry powder

¼ cup sugar

½ cup dry white wine

6 tablespoons white wine vinegar

Salt

A large saucepan

Canning jars and lids

Chop the onions very finely. Cook them in the melted butter until they are golden, but not brown. Peel and shred the ginger, and thinly slice the banana. Add the ginger, the banana, the curry, the sugar, and the salt to the onions. Cook the mixture slightly before sprinkling with the white wine and the vinegar. Cook, uncovered, for twenty to thirty minutes, stirring regularly. Taste, adding salt if necessary. Fill small jars with the very hot mixture, and close them immediately.

Pascale Goldenberg, Germany

Tomato Chutney

2 lbs. tomatoes, scalded, peeled, and chopped

2 medium-sized onions, thinly sliced

3 apples, peeled and diced

1½ cups brown sugar

½ cup raisins

2 cups cider vinegar

1 tablespoon salt

½ teaspoon black pepper

2 cloves garlic, crushed

2 cayenne peppers, dried and finely chopped

6 cloves

1 teaspoon ground cinnamon

An enamel or stainless steel saucepan

Canning jars and lids

This chutney is particularly good to make at the end of the season, as it allows you to use not-too-ripe (or even green) tomatoes and apples that have fallen to the ground.

Prepare all the ingredients and put them in an enamel or stainless steel pan. Slowly bring to a boil and continue simmering over low heat, uncovered. Stir from time to time. The mixture will gradually thicken; when done, it should resemble a thick jam. This could take up to three hours or more.

Put the chutney into jars. Close and store in a cool, dry place.

Jeannette Busiaux, L'Étang-la-Ville

KETCHUP AND OTHER VEGETABLE CONDIMENTS

Ketchup with Little Added Sugar

12 to 13 lbs. tomatoes, very ripe

3 large onions, chopped

2 green peppers, seeded and chopped

1 clove garlic (or more, to taste)

1⅞ cups sugar

1¾ cups cider vinegar

1 heaping tablespoon salt

1 tablespoon sweet paprika

1 tablespoon dry mustard

A large saucepan

A fine strainer

Canning jars and lids

SACHET CONTAINING:

1 cinnamon stick

1 teaspoon black peppercorns

1 teaspoon Jamaica peppers (or allspice)

1 dried hot chili pepper

1 tablespoon cloves

1 teaspoon fennel or celery seeds

Cook the tomatoes, onions, green peppers, and garlic for forty-five minutes, or until very tender.

Pass the mixture through a fine strainer to remove the tomato peels and seeds, but collect as much pulp as possible. Add the remaining ingredients and the spice sachet to the pulp. Simmer everything over low heat for two to three hours, stirring regularly, until the mixture is thick. Remove the spice sachet.

To sterilize the jars before filling them, I place them in the oven and heat them for a few minutes. Put the very hot ketchup into the jars, and immediately close them airtight. Store in a dark, cool place.

Yields two to two-and-a-half quarts.

Anonymous

Honey Ketchup

4 lbs. tomatoes, very ripe

1 or 2 sweet peppers (optional)

1 teaspoon marjoram

1 teaspoon basil

1 teaspoon cayenne pepper

1 teaspoon ground cloves

1 pinch nutmeg

1 tablespoon paprika

1 teaspoon salt

4 tablespoons honey

1 cup wine vinegar

A large saucepan

A strainer

Canning jars and lids

Chop the tomatoes and the sweet peppers. Add the other ingredients and cook over low heat for thirty minutes, stirring from time to time. Strain; then cook over low heat for another hour to reduce. Pour the mixture, while still very hot, into scalded glass jars (eight or sixteen ounces). Seal immediately.

Jeanne Régisser, Sundhoffen

Homemade Piccalilli Relish

6½ lbs. vegetables (depending on availability): cauliflower, zucchini, celery, sweet pepper, pearl onion, cucumber, gherkin, green bean, young carrot

1 lb. salt (to draw moisture from the vegetables)

SWEET-AND-SOUR SAUCE:

   1 tablespoon curcuma [turmeric]

   4 teaspoons mustard

   4 teaspoons ground ginger

   1⅞ cups sugar

   1¾ quarts vinegar (save 3 tablespoons)

   3 tablespoons cornstarch (save with the 3 tablespoons of vinegar)

or

SPICIER SAUCE:

   1 tablespoon curcuma [turmeric]

   8 teaspoons mustard

   8 teaspoons ground ginger

   1¼ cups sugar

   1¼ quarts vinegar (save 3 tablespoons)

   1½ tablespoons cornstarch (save with the 3 tablespoons of vinegar)

A terrine

A large saucepan

A skimmer

Canning jars and lids

Chop the vegetables into small pieces and put them in a terrine, alternating with the salt. Let them sit for twenty-four hours. Rinse and carefully drain the vegetables. Prepare either the sweet-and-sour or the spicier sauce by combining all the listed ingredients, except the withheld vinegar and cornstarch, in a large saucepan. Add the drained vegetables and simmer for one hour; do not overcook (doneness depends on your taste).

When the vegetables are ready, remove them with a skimmer and put them in jars that have already been sterilized in the oven. Add the cornstarch, diluted in the three tablespoons of vinegar, to the sauce, and let it thicken for three minutes. Pour the sauce over the vegetables, and close the jars immediately. Wait six weeks before using.

Mrs. Besale, Belgium

Sweet-and-Sour Pickles

Cucumbers
1 ½ tablespoons salt
1 ½ tablespoons sugar
Tarragon
Parsley
Garlic
White pearl onions
2 cups vinegar
1-quart canning jar and lid

Use fresh cucumbers; wash and dry them.

In a one-quart jar, combine all the ingredients, except for the vinegar. Boil a mixture of equal parts water and vinegar. Pour this over the cucumbers while they still are hot, and close the jar immediately.

J. Devillers, Pont-de-Roide

Sweet-and-Sour Tomato Coulis

22 lbs. red tomatoes
3 lbs. onions
1 ½ quarts cider vinegar
2 lbs. sugar
3 tablespoons salt
3 tablespoons ground pepper
1 teaspoon paprika
2 teaspoons ground ginger
1 teaspoon four-spices [allspice]
1 teaspoon curry powder
3 teaspoons mustard
1 fresh nutmeg, grated
A food mill
A large stockpot
A wooden spoon
Canning jars and lids

Slice the tomatoes; peel and thinly slice the onions. Cook these vegetables together for twenty minutes. Next, put them through a food mill, pouring the purée into a large stockpot. Reduce the purée over heat, stirring with a wooden spoon. Add the vinegar, sugar, and all the spices, and cook for about another twenty minutes. Let cool; then use a funnel to transfer the coulis to jars, preferably widemouthed ones.

VARIATION:

You can make the same recipe without onions, and substitute wine vinegar for cider vinegar.

Eric and Sylvie Courtille, Lacapelle-Marival

SWEET-AND-SOUR FRUITS

Cherries in Vinegar

2 lbs. cherries (English,
   'Montmorency', or
   'Napoleon')

¾ cup sugar

1 cinnamon stick

A few cloves

Lemon rind

White wine vinegar

Scissors

A wooden toothpick

Canning jar and lid

Use only very healthy cherries. With scissors, cut the stems, leaving about one-quarter inch on the fruit. Pierce each cherry with a wooden toothpick, and put them all in a scalded glass jar. Sprinkle the cherries with the sugar; then add a few cloves, the lemon rind, and the cinnamon stick. Boil enough white wine vinegar to fill the jar. Let it cool, and pour it over the cherries. Close the jar tightly, and store in a dark place for two months.

Serve these cherries as an appetizer, or as a side dish for grilled meat and beef stew. They are very tasty with Christmas turkey (without stuffing). Once you finish them, you have a delicious cherry vinegar to enjoy.

Josiane Leralu, Canada

'Schmidt's Bigarreau' Cherries in Vinegar

2 lbs. 'Schmidt's
   Bigarreau' cherries

1 quart cider vinegar

1¾ cups sugar (or less, to
   taste)

3 cloves

2 bay leaves

¼ of a cinnamon stick

A stoneware pot or glass
   jar and lid

A clean cloth

An enamel saucepan

Waxed paper

Cut the stems to a half-inch long; wash and dry the cherries. Scald a stoneware pot or a glass jar, and wipe with a clean cloth.

Put the cherries in the pot, packing them lightly. Boil the vinegar, the sugar, and the spices in an enamel saucepan. Pour this, while hot, over the cherries. Line the cover of the pot (or jar lid) with waxed paper, and close the jar.

Like pickles, the cherries will be ready to eat after two months. Serve them with cold cuts, terrines, or salads.

Josiane Leralu, Canada

Marinated Red Fruit

Fruit: morello cherries,
   gooseberries, red
   currants, green grapes

MARINADE:

Vinegar

Sugar (5 cubes [2–3
   tablespoons] per 2
   cups of vinegar) or
   honey

Orange rind

Cloves

Cinnamon

A covered pan

Canning jars and lids

In the area around Nice [southeastern France], we eat ham with melon and marinated red fruit.

Boil the marinade slowly in a covered pan for five minutes. Let cool. Put the fruit into clean jars (avoid metal lids, which vinegar corrodes). Pour the marinade over the fruit, making sure there are no air bubbles, and close the jars. Store in a cool cellar; they will keep for at least one year. Refrigerate the jars after opening.

Serve this fruit with ham, beef stew, or steak tartare. You can also use it as a stuffing for cakes. Delicious!

VARIATION:

The same recipe can be prepared using any garden vegetables, particularly very firm cherry tomatoes. Purslane also keeps well this way (use white vinegar diluted in a little water to retain its green color).

Anne-Marie Arrouye, Aix-en-Provence

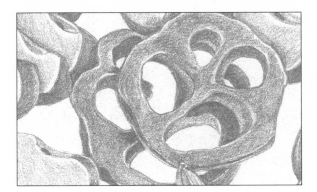

Dessert Pears in Vinegar

2 lbs. sugar
2 cups vinegar
8¾ lbs. ripe cooking pears
A large saucepan
A stoneware pot or
 canning jars
Plastic wrap or lids

Combine the vinegar and the sugar in a large pan. Cook over low heat until the sugar dissolves. Arrange the whole pears, peeled but still with their stems, in layers in the pan. Boil, covered, over low heat for three hours, and then uncovered, for an additional three hours. Do not stir. Then, holding the pears by their stems, transfer them to jars or a stoneware pot. Cover the pears with the remaining syrup. Seal the jars as you would for jams, with plastic wrap or lids. The pears will keep as long as jam.

Pascale Dey-Marquis, Montigny-en-Gohelle

VARIATION:

Add one or two cinnamon sticks and a few cloves. Some recipes require less cooking: one and a half hours covered, followed by one hour uncovered.

Jacqueline Closset, Belgium

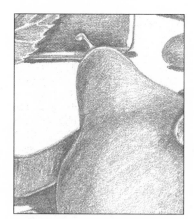

Sweet-and-Sour Dark Red Plums

6½ lbs. firm dark red plums (not too ripe)

2 lbs. sugar

2 cups white vinegar (or 3 cups, if you prefer more sour than sweet)

2 cups water

¼ oz. cinnamon sticks

4–6 cloves

A knitting needle (or the point of a knife)

Canning jars and lids

Wash the plums and pierce the skin three to six times, using a knitting needle (or the point of a knife). Boil the other ingredients and let them cool. Put the fruit into the liquid to soak overnight.

The next day, remove the fruit, and bring the liquid to a boil again. Let it cool, and put the fruit back in to soak for twenty-four hours.

Remove the fruit once again, and then boil the liquid one last time. Taste carefully; if necessary, add more water and vinegar. Pour the boiling liquid over the fruit. Let this stand for three days; then put it in jars.

Dark red plums can be replaced by morello cherries in this recipe. The fruit can be served alone, as an appetizer; as a complement to game, or beef stew; or as a remedy for all sorts of excesses (it settles the stomach).

Béatrice Sommer, Pfaffenhoffen

Sweet-and-Sour Plums

2 cups white vinegar (or 3 cups, if you prefer more sour than sweet)

2 cups water

6½ lbs. plums (not too ripe)

2 lbs. sugar

¼ oz. cinnamon sticks

4–6 cloves

A large saucepan

A skimmer

A stoneware pot or glass jar

A piece cheesecloth

White paper

Boil the vinegar and water. Put the plums in the boiling liquid and continue to boil for five minutes. Remove the plums with a skimmer and transfer them to a stoneware pot, or a glass jar. Boil the liquid again, and pour it over the plums. Cover the pot with a cheesecloth and let this stand for two or three days.

Next, drain and boil some liquid again for a few minutes, and pour it back over the plums. Wait until everything cools before covering the pot with white paper. Store all winter in the cellar.

This recipe and the one for pears in vinegar (see page 170) are both traditional Walloon recipes, given to me by my grandmother. They are well known around the countryside, and are served with pork, rabbit, and even roasted chicken.

Jacqueline Closset, Belgium

Chapter 9

PRESERVING IN ALCOHOL

PRESERVING
IN ALCOHOL

DOES THIS PRESERVATION METHOD
have its place in a book on "healthy"
ways to preserve food? It all depends on the use. Alcohol appears to be
one of the most effective means to preserve certain medicinal plants. And, as
for other foods stored in wine or other
alcohol, it goes without saying that
moderation is recommended.

FLAVORED WINES

Dandelion Wine

3 quarts dandelion flowers
1½ lbs. honey or 2 lbs.
   sugar
Rind and juice of 2
   oranges
Rind and juice of 1 lemon
2 cloves
2 cardamom pods
Stale bread
Baker's yeast
A ceramic pot
Bottles and corks

Pick three quarts of dandelion flowers. Soak them immediately in four quarts of boiling water, and let them sit in this water for three days.

After three days, filter the liquid. Add to it the rind from the two oranges and the lemon, along with the sugar or honey. Boil this mixture for fifteen minutes. Turn the heat off, and add the juice from the oranges and the lemon. Stir in two cloves and two cardamom pods. Simmer slowly for thirty minutes.

Filter and pour the liquid into a ceramic pot. Add to this some stale bread that has been spread with baker's yeast. Ferment for two weeks. Then pour it into bottles, carefully seal them tight, and wait a few months before using.

Pierre Perlati, Deluz

Elderberry Wine

11 lbs. elderberries
1 lb. sugar
1 lb. honey
1 pinch salt
A strainer or food mill
A large container with a
   cover
Bottles and lids

Crush out the juice from the elderberries. In a large container, combine the elderberry juice with the sugar, the honey, and the salt. Close the container and let it stand for one month. Then pour the wine into bottles. Seal.

Michel Guerville, Dannes

Elderflower Wine

Elderflowers
Sweet white wine
Bottles and lids

Layer the bottom of a bottle with elderflowers. Fill with a sweet white wine. Soak for eight days and then filter the wine into another bottle. Seal.

Michel Guerville, Dannes

May Wine

❧ Sweet woodruff *(Asperula odorata)* grows beneath deciduous trees (beeches especially). It blooms from May to June. May wine is reputed to aid in digestion.

A large handful of sweet woodruff
1 quart white wine (Sylvaner or Riesling)
½ cup sugar
Bottles and corks

As you walk through the woods in the month of May, prepare to concoct this invigorating tonic. Pick the sweet woodruff when it begins to flower. Soak it in the white wine, mixed with the sugar for one month. Then filter and pour the liquid into bottles. Serve this aperitif very chilled.

Elsie Bohr, Strasbourg

Walnut Wine

4 quarts good red wine

2 cups distilled grape marc (*grappa*)

40 green walnuts (picked at the end of June, beginning of July)

Cinnamon

Vanilla

1 lb. sugar

A demijohn

Bottle(s) and cork(s)

Pour the wine and the grape marc into a demijohn. Quarter the nuts, and put them in the demijohn, along with a bit of cinnamon and vanilla. Let stand for two months. Filter the wine and add the sugar. The longer you age it, the better the wine will be.

This aperitif is well liked and does not contain too much alcohol.

A. Dijoud, St. Joseph-de-Rivière

VARIATIONS:

You can replace the grape marc with some other brandy, and use a rosé wine, or a mixture of dry white wine and red wine. Some recipes recommend soaking the nuts in brandy only (from forty days to one year, depending on the recipe), adding the wine at the same time as the sugar, after having filtered the brandy. The cinnamon and vanilla are optional.

Wild Raspberry Wine

4 quarts good-quality white wine

2 cups distilled grape marc (*grappa*)

1 lb. wild raspberries

Cinnamon

Vanilla

1 lb. sugar

Demijohn

Bottle(s) and cork(s)

Use the same recipe as for walnut wine above, but with white wine instead. Replace the nuts with one pound of wild raspberries (more flavor than cultivated raspberries).

A. Dijoud and J. Richel, St. Joseph-de-Rivière

FRUITS PRESERVED IN ALCOHOL

Officer's "Jam" or Bachelor's Liqueur

✤ This recipe is not recommended for those on a diet; however, we can indulge ourselves once in a while!

Fruit (whatever's available): strawberries, red currants, black currants, wild raspberries, peaches, plums, greengage plums, apricots, etc.

Alcohol: kirsch for red fruit, cognac for others, or brandy for everything (but kirsch or cognac are best)

Sugar (same quantity as the fruit)

5-quart stoneware pot with lid

This "jam" is prepared as the fruit ripens, over the course of the growing season.

Cut larger fruit into smaller pieces, and remove all pits. Then, in a very large, airtight stoneware pot (called a *Rumtopf* in Switzerland), alternate layers of one pound of fruit and one pound of sugar, as the harvest continues. Personally, I use less sugar: I cover each layer of fruit with sugar, without weighing it first. It keeps as well as the version with more sugar.

Each time you add more fruit, cover it with the alcohol you've selected. Never stir. Store the pot in a cool, dark place, and wait at least six months before tasting this delicacy. However, it's much better if you wait one year.

Mrs. Defacqz, Switzerland

Dried Apricots in Brandy

3⅓ lbs. dried apricots
1 vanilla bean
Brandy
2 tablespoons sugar
2 cups water
A saucepan
Canning jar and lid

Pour about one-half inch of brandy into a jar; then add the apricots, in layers, inserting several ¼-inch pieces of vanilla bean here and there. Fill the jar to one and a quarter inches below the rim. Make a syrup in a saucepan, using two cups of water and dissolving the sugar over low heat. Let this cool and pour it over the fruit. Close the jar airtight, and shake gently to mix the sugar and the brandy.

Store the apricots in a dark, dry place; wait two months before eating them (patience!). They will keep indefinitely.

Jean-Yves Cousseau, Millau

Prunes in Brandy

2 lbs. prunes

FOR THE LINDEN TEA:
A handful of dried linden flowers
3 cups water
A jar
A saucepan

FOR THE SYRUP:
1 quart brandy
24 cubes of sugar [¾ cup]
1 cup water

Make a linden tea by steeping the linden flowers in three cups of water. Filter this and soak the prunes in the tea for twelve hours.

Drain the prunes and put them in a jar. Over low heat, make a syrup using the twenty-four cubes of sugar and one cup of water. Pour this over the prunes, and then cover them well with brandy. Seal the jar.

Wait fifteen days before eating. These prunes will keep indefinitely.

Jean-Yves Cousseau, Millau

Prunes in Wine

2 lbs. medium-sized
  prunes
Linden tea (see p. 180)
1½ cups sugar
1 quart of not-too-strong,
  good red wine
  (Bordeaux, Bergerac,
  etc.)
1 cup brandy
A large jar and lid

Preserving fruit in alcohol is not encouraged much these days. Still, here is a recipe that is very popular among my friends. Remember, however, one prune is enough.

Soak the prunes overnight in the linden tea. Drain and sort them. (Immediately eat those that might not hold up.) Put the prunes in a large jar, add the sugar, and cover completely with the wine and the brandy. (Add more wine, if necessary.) Close the jar, shaking it a little to help dissolve the sugar.

Store the prunes in a dark closet for at least two months. Enjoy! These prunes can be used to dress up certain desserts (fruit salads, puddings, and so on).

Brigitte Lapouge-Dejean, Domme

Raspberries in Brandy

Raspberries
Plain brandy
2½ cups sugar
A saucepan
Canning jar and lid

Fill a jar halfway with plain brandy. Add ripe but firm whole raspberries as you pick them. When the jar is full, close it and let it stand for forty days.

Add the following liqueur-like syrup: Put the sugar (about two and a half cups of sugar per one quart of brandy) in a saucepan with a bit of water. Let the sugar slowly dissolve until it becomes an opaque white. Allow this syrup to cool before pouring it over the raspberries.

The raspberries remain whole. They're delicious and can be served as a garnish for ice cream.

Christine Moulinier, Sadirac

Sun-Cooked Cherries in Brandy

1 quart cherries
('Schmidt's Bigarreau',
for example)
½ cup sugar
½ cup brandy
1-quart canning jar and lid
(new rubber seal)

If possible, leave the cherries unwashed. Cut the stems to half an inch long. Fill a one-quart jar right to the rim with cherries, packing them well. Add the sugar, then the brandy, and close the jar with a new rubber seal. Leave the jar out in the sun for one month, or longer if the weather is cloudy. Shake the jar after one week of solar "cooking."

Eat the cherries within two years, but be careful: This is not a dessert!

Georges Dutreix, Mondouzil

WHICH METHOD FOR PRESERVING EACH FOOD?

T HE FOLLOWING TABLE IS A GUIDE-line to preservation methods for the foods mentioned in this book. We have differentiated the basic methods, which are used the most often and, in our opinion, are the most interesting, from other suitable methods. For some foods, no basic method is recommended. This means that the food should be eaten while fresh, and that the methods shown are only of occasional interest.

	METHOD	Whole (ground, silo, cellar, etc.)	Drying	Lactic Fermentation	Oil	Vinegar	Salt	Sugar	Sweet-and-Sour	Alcohol
◆ = Basic ● = Alternate										
All-Year Radish				●						
Anchovy						◆	◆			
Angelica								◆		●
Animal fat		◆								
Apricot			◆					◆		●
Artichoke			●		●					
Ash fruit								◆		●
Banana			●							
Basil					◆	●				
Black currant			●					◆		
Black salsify		◆								
Blackberry								◆		
Blueberry		◆	●							
Bread			●							
Brussels sprout		◆				●				
Cardoon			●							
Carob								◆		
Carrot		◆		●						
Cauliflower		◆								
Cherry			●			●			●	●
Chervil								●		
Chestnut		◆	◆							
Chutney									◆	
Cottage cheese					◆					
Cucumber				◆						
Curly kale		◆								
Dandelion flower										●
Dry vegetables		◆								
Egg		●				●				
Eggplant			●	●	●					

	METHOD	Whole (ground, silo, cellar, etc.)	Drying	Lactic Fermentation	Oil	Vinegar	Salt	Sugar	Sweet-and-Sour	Alcohol
◆ = Basic ● = Alternate										
Elderberry								◆		●
Elderflower										●
Endive		◆								
Fish			◆							
Garlic		◆				●				
Gherkin				◆		◆			●	
Glasswort						◆				
Goat cheese					◆					
Grape			◆			●				
Grape Leaves							◆			
Green bean			◆	◆			◆			
Gruyère cheese		◆								
Herring						◆				
Hot pepper			◆		●					
Jerusalem artichoke		◆								
Ketchup									◆	
Lamb's lettuce		◆								
Leek		◆								
Lemon							●			
Lettuce				●						
Melon								◆		
Mixed vegetables				◆						
Mushroom			◆		●	●				
Nasturtium (seeds)						◆				
Olive		●			●					
Onion		◆	●	●		●				
Orach			●							
Parsnip		◆								
Peach			●							
Pear		◆	◆					●	●	

	METHOD	Whole (ground, silo, cellar, etc.)	Drying	Lactic Fermentation	Oil	Vinegar	Salt	Sugar	Sweet-and-Sour	Alcohol
◆ = Basic ● = Alternate										
Persimmon			●							
Plum			◆	◆		●		◆	●	
Prune		●								●
Raspberry			●					◆		●
Red beet			●	◆						
Red cabbage		◆								
Red currant			●					◆		
Rhubarb		◆						●		
Rose petals							●			
Rosehip								◆		
Salsify		◆								
Sea buckthorn berry								◆		
Spinach			●							
Squash		◆								
Strawberry			●					◆		
Sweet pepper			●			●				
Sweet woodruff										◆
Swiss chard			●	◆						
Tomatillos						●				
Tomato		◆	◆	●	●	●	●		●	
Turnip		◆		◆						
Walnuts		◆								
White cabbage		◆		◆						
Whortleberries		◆	●							
Wild vegetables			●							
Winter radish		◆		●						
Yeast			●							
Zucchini			●	●	●					

❧ INDEX ❦

CHELSEA GREEN

Sustainable living has many facets. Chelsea Green's celebration of the sustainable arts has led us to publish trend-setting books about organic gardening, solar electricity and renewable energy, innovative building techniques, regenerative forestry, local and bioregional democracy, and whole foods. The company's published works, while intensely practical, are also entertaining and inspirational, demonstrating that an ecological approach to life is consistent with producing beautiful, eloquent, and useful books, videos, and audio cassettes.

For more information about Chelsea Green, or to request a free catalog, call toll-free (800) 639-4099, or write to us at P.O. Box 428, White River Junction, Vermont 05001. Visit our Web site at www.chelseagreen.com.

Chelsea Green's titles include:

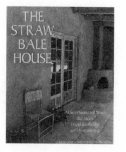 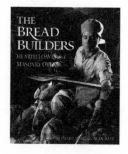 

The Straw Bale House	The Bread Builders	Gaviotas
The New Independent Home	Whole Foods Companion	Loving and Leaving the
Independent Builder:	Simple Food for the	Good Life
Designing & Building a	Good Life	Scott Nearing: The Making
House Your Own Way	The Apple Grower	of a Homesteader
The Rammed Earth House	The Flower Farmer	Who Owns the Sun?
The Passive Solar House	Passport to Gardening	Global Spin:
The Earth-Sheltered House	The New Organic Grower	The Corporate Assault
The Sauna	Four-Season Harvest	on Environmentalism
Wind Energy Basics	Solar Gardening	Hemp Horizons
The Solar Living Sourcebook	Straight-Ahead Organic	Beyond the Limits
A Shelter Sketchbook	The Contrary Farmer	The Man Who Planted Trees
Mortgage-Free!	The Contrary Farmer's	The Northern Forest
Hammer. Nail. Wood.	Invitation to Gardening	Seeing Nature
Stone Circles	Good Spirits	Believing Cassandra